ATTITUDES

OF

AMAZING

ACHIEVERS

PHILIP BAKER

From the author of the Best Seller SECRETS OF SUPER ACHIEVERS

BY THE SAME AUTHOR

Secrets of Super Achievers

Wisdom - The Forgotten Factor of Success

ATTITUDES OF AMAZING ACHIEVERS

All enquiries regarding this publication to:-

Catalyst Books
13 New Row
Covent Garden, London
WC2N 4LF
Tel: 0207 380 4646
Fax: 0207 380 4647

Printed by Redwood Books, Trowbridge, Wiltshire.
National Library of Australia, Canberra, Australia
ISBN 0957702000

DEDICATION

To my three mums

Teresa

Val and

Pat

THANKS

The evolution of a book is a wonderful thing. All I do is put words together using my trusty pen and paper. (I am still able to resist the allure of Wordperfect 1.0 - have they improved upon that yet?) Yet from those barely legible pages a book has sprung. Thanks are mainly due to Penny who after years of preparation deciphering ancient coptic and Mesopotamian scrolls is now able to roughly translate my meanderings into some pretty good stuff... which often bears no relation to what I actually wrote.

Thanks are also due to my wife, Heather, and three totally pliable, incredibly placid girls - NOT! who allow me to head for the mountains once or twice a year to write.

I would also like to thank the staff and partners of Riverview. The privilege of working week-by-week in a local church is the best environment I know to form character, find meaning and, of course, develop the kind of attitudes that give life its richness.

CONTENTS

DISCLAIMER

Well I am already having second thoughts... I have just realised that in writing a book about attitude I have set myself up. If at any time in the future I have a bad attitude about anything, everyone close to me is going to be quick to point out the fact that I wrote a book about this and maybe I should go and read it! So let me say at the outset that there are several things that I reserve the right to have a bad attitude about:

NUMBER 1

Running out of any type of sauce when it is absolutely necessary to complete a meal. I have been known to drive for half an hour to buy that underestimated yet vital bottle of mint sauce to complement the lamb. Other 'must-haves' in my life are horseradish with beef, soya sauce for sushi, and béarnaise sauce with fresh asparagus.

Number 2

Running out of washer water in my car and watching as the last bit dribbles onto the screen smudging the grime into complex yet unappreciated patterns that then require an unscheduled stop at a service station.

Number 3

Unscheduled stops at service stations. I hate stopping for fuel. The sooner someone designs an on-the-road fueling vehicle much like they have for airplanes, the better.

Number 4

The way the creepy-crawly pool cleaner concentrates 95% of its effort in one corner, and like a boomerang returns to it the moment I have pulled it to the other end.

Number 5

Drivers who decide to change lanes and don't indicate until they are actually in motion. Or even worse, drivers who decide to make a turn at lights and fail to put the indicator on until you are trapped right behind them.

Number 6

Asking my wife what I have a bad attitude about and having her go on and on and on...!

I reserve the right, as the author of this work, to maintain these pathetic and self-serving attitudes even though they constitute a major diversion from the thrust of this volume. I trust the reader will so indulge me and that the credibility I thus lose through hypocrisy, I will gain back for honesty and vulnerability.

SECTION I

THE ANATOMY OF ATTITUDE

CHAPTER 1

ON CRICKET, IMPATIENCE AND GRANDFATHER CLOCKS

'THE IMPORTANCE OF ATTITUDE'

'A HAPPY PERSON IS NOT A PERSON IN A CERTAIN SET OF CIRCUMSTANCES BUT RATHER A PERSON WITH A CERTAIN SET OF ATTITUDES.'

HUGH DOWNS

I must confess I have been procrastinating. Today has been set aside to begin writing my new book. The book you are now holding in your hands. Yet today is also the fourth day of the first test match between Australia and England. I love cricket and so I have been sitting in my car, notebook at hand, vowing after each over to turn the radio off. It was not until one of the commentators made the statement, "it all comes down to attitude," that I realised I needed to get to work. The reason I want to write on this subject is because the commentator was right. . . it all does come down to attitude.

The importance of attitude is not, however, merely a cliché, mentioned glibly at sporting events. The longer I live, the more I study and experience, the more I am convinced of the primacy of attitude. Yet, how many of us really believe this? Our educational systems focus on knowledge, our political systems on manoeuvring, and our job resumes detail our competence. Libraries are filled with volumes on how to develop one's IQ, memory, practical knowledge and specific skills, yet there is hardly a volume that details the specifics of attitude. Make a visit to your local library and type 'attitude' into the key word catalogue of the computer. You are likely to pull up one or two fiction books, maybe a Mills and Boon romance, <u>An Attitude of Love</u>, and several non-fiction works which have thrown the word into their title but are mainly written about horticulture, lighthouse keeping or sail boat racing. If it does all come down to attitude, why is there so little information on this vital subject?

One of the problems is, of course, that attitude is intangible. It is difficult to come to grips with, to define or explain. It hides behind our weaknesses and our strengths. So when someone's problem really is their attitude, they are quick to posit many other excuses which sound and look more solid, but are camouflaging the real culprit. I am convinced that attitude in life is 'the' critical ingredient. Like meat to bolognese, vermouth to martini, or chicken to KFC. One can succeed in life without a huge lot of knowledge or connections if one has developed a healthy, successful attitude.

A

On the other hand, the negative, the sloppy, the mediocre, the half-hearted, the self-proclaimed victims, the stingy, the sour and the arrogant are quick to point their finger to the multiple circumstances of life which have kept them down. They do not realise that it is their own interpretation and interactions with life's journey that is the anchor around their ankles, frustrating their dreams and diminishing their destiny. The greedy are hard done by, the proud never find deep relationships, the selfish are always aware of what they don't have, the negative are mindful of the light fading and so consequently miss the wonderful colours of the sunset. Life is the same for all of us; it has its ups and downs, its pain and pleasure.

Yet our attitude is the one thing we have within our control. It gives us the power of understanding, of perspective and self-mastery. It was Oscar Wilde who said that, *'all of us are lying in the gutter but some of us are looking at the stars.'* Yet the right kind of attitude actually has within it the power to change the story, to create opportunities, to win favour from friends and promotions from employers. It gives

A

us the power to rejoice in the little things and to celebrate the simple moments. Our attitude towards the passing of time, for example, will change the way we get out of bed in the morning or celebrate our fortieth birthday. Time can be wonderful or terrible, not based on what we are doing but on our attitude to what we are doing.

I was recently on holiday with my family in the Catskill Mountains of New York. Snow had been falling for most of the morning as we pulled into a quaint New England town and visited a local historic hotel. We were about to walk down the street, visiting the local shops when my six-year-old daughter put in a request to visit the ladies' restrooms (although she didn't exactly use that terminology). I agreed to wait outside while my wife and other daughter began to walk down the road. The reader should know that I hate waiting. I constantly change lines in customs or supermarket lanes to minimise waiting time. I prefer to drive forty minutes out of my way to avoid a traffic jam, rather than sit ten minutes in stationary traffic. So I sat down impatiently on the sofa in the small lobby waiting for my daughter to reappear. A fire was burning in the hearth, a light snow was falling, visible from the window which overlooked a small pine forest, yet my eye was not on my surroundings, but on the fact that I wanted to be doing something else. After three or four minutes my impatience got the better of me; I went to the door of the toilets and called out, 'Temily, are you okay?' To which the reply came back, 'Yes, Daddy, I'm just doing poohs!' It took fifteen minutes for my daughter to finish her business. Fifteen minutes! I thought at the time that this must be some kind of record. I was frustrated, agitated and irritated. I did not live those fifteen minutes. I lost them in a haze of rush — induced myopia. Yet a month later when I was back in Australia, I thought of how I had missed out on that fifteen minutes of life. I would have done almost anything to be sitting again on that sofa watching the fire burn and the snow fall, enjoying myself while I waited for my daughter. The difference was not what I was doing but my interpretation of it.

On the same holiday I had an opportunity to redeem myself. This time I was sitting in a bed-and-breakfast lounge; it was mid-

A

afternoon. Again the fire was burning in the hearth, a light snow was falling outside and the gentle ticking of a grandfather clock completed the picture. Temily came into the room and sat up on my lap and we began to talk. I pointed out the grandfather clock and asked her if she had seen one before. She hadn't and so I began to explain to her that a grandfather clock makes different kinds of chimes at different times of the hour. Seeing the time was five to three, we decided to sit and listen to the three o'clock tune. This we both greatly enjoyed and the conversation quickly turned to, 'what kind of sound the clock would make at quarter-past?' I pointed out that a good grandfather clock would make a different sound at quarter-past than it does at the o'clock or the half-past mark. So we sat and listened to the quarter-past and then the half-past and then simply had to stay to see if the quarter-to differed in any way from the quarter-past. Now, if you had asked me to sit in a chair and watch a grandfather clock for an hour I would have been quick to inform you that this would be my idea of nothing to do . . . along with washing dishes, mowing lawns or measuring maggots for a school assignment. Yet, I more than just enjoyed that hour . . . I loved that hour.

A few months later I was talking to Temily about our holiday. 'Do you remember when we sat in the chair and watched the clock?' I asked.

Her eyes lit up and a smile erupted on her face, 'Yes, Dad. That was great.' In my daughter's estimation it was up there with Disneyland and skiing. You see, life is not about what happens but what we think about what happens. It is not about how bad things are, it is about how we interpret our circumstances, and whether or not we decide to learn lessons or wallow in self-pity. Attitude not only gives us a better view from the gutter, but also gives us the power to get out of it, to walk tall, straight, with a skip in our step and a determination to savour the God-given gift of life.

CHAPTER 2

YOUR ATTITUDE IS SHOWING

'FIVE THINGS ATTITUDE DOES'

It may help us to grasp the importance of attitude if we break down its intangibility and look at some of the results that attitude creates in our lives.

NUMBER 1
ATTITUDE DETERMINES PERSPECTIVE

Attitude affects how we see things. Things are rarely seen as they actually are. We view our world through the prism of our

A

understanding, experience, feelings and attitudes. William Blake makes this point well, *'This life's dim windows of the soul distorts the heavens from pole to pole and leads you to believe a lie when you see with, not thro', the eye.'*[1]

We understand anatomically that we don't see with the eye. We see with the brain. Our attitude is that which interprets the image. So we begin to get what we look for. We see what we want to see. 'Red cars travel together.' The first time I heard this particular phrase was on a comedy radio programme. My first reaction was of course to laugh at such a patently false suggestion. And yet in the next few days I came to the realisation it was true! Wherever I looked I saw red cars together. Now of course, I was selectively seeing, screening out the lone red cars and only noticing when they travelled in packs. Thus what I believed became reality and that reality convinced me of what I believed. In the same way the victim in life interprets everything in line with the belief that everybody and everything is against them. The person who declares all politicians are crooked only notices those who are, and conveniently ignores

A

those who are not. The atheist is quick to point out reasons and evidences of the non-existence of God, and begins to selectively view the world, consequently finding it almost impossible to see arguments on the other side. The Christian on the other hand often only looks at the good declaring there has to be a God without really considering the arguments of the agnostic.

My point is, that life is. It is how we view that differs. The glass is both half full and half empty at the same time.

There will always be rain and sunshine. Yet if we choose to hate the rain we are choosing to be miserable for a good proportion of our lives, not because it is raining, but because we choose to not enjoy the fact that it is raining. Others have the attitude that things will only be good if there is a lot of money in the bank. This is clung to despite the fact that case study after case study has proven that happiness and fulfilment have little to do with net worth.

I always marvel at those who have had serious setbacks in life, physically disabled or emotionally damaged, yet choose to be grateful for who they are and what they have. Those who are disadvantaged and yet celebrate the passing of each minute as a gift from God, are those who inspire humanity. The man with no legs who ran across Canada to raise money; the quadriplegic who spends time travelling and inspiring high-school students. The Christopher Reeves and the Forrest Gumps of our world teach a powerful truth: that life is what you make of it and that those of us who actually have a whole lot going for us should not spend a single moment in complaining, regret or self-induced pity. Rather we should be grateful and realise that joy comes not from the weather, the bank account or the place of our abode, but from far more significant things like relationships, spirituality and attitude.

NUMBER 2
ATTITUDE REFLECTS OUR RELATIONAL HISTORY

Family of origin, peer group pressure, high school gangs, all affect who we are.

A

Those who tend to see the negative before they see the positive are often reflecting the household they grew up in. When gossiping or small-minded people surround you in your formative years, it takes incredible strength of character and openness of vision to break out of the cycle. We tend to inherit our political, religious and social view of life from others. We catch what they have got. This can, of course, be both good and bad. Yet, attitude formation and cultivation should not be left to rest on such haphazard and arbitrary ground.

It is, of course, the contention of this book, that regardless of one's upbringing we can all change our attitudes.

Let me also say that it is very easy to underestimate the power of peer pressure. 'Group think' can become such a powerful thing that it is almost impossible to escape its centripetal force. The current runs strong and only the vigorous will survive in their upstream quest. Professor Stanley Milgram has done a variety of experiments on the phenomena of peer pressure... showing the incredible pains it takes to go against society's norms. In

A

one such experiment he asked one of his students to go up to different people on the subway train and request that that person give up their seat to them without giving an explanation as to the why. This task was meant to be conducted with twenty strangers, gauging their different reactions. After trying this a couple of times the student backed out declaring that it was the most difficult thing he had ever had to do in his life! Milgram decided to take over and conduct the experiment himself. As he approached the first person he found himself sweating and shaking, almost to the point of extreme panic. He asked for the seat and found the person gave it to him.

> *'Taking the man's seat I was overwhelmed by the need to behave in a way to justify my request. My head sank between my knees and I could feel my face blanching. I was not role-playing. I actually felt as if I was going to perish. As soon as I got off the train, all tension disappeared.'* [2]

It is essential, therefore, to try to get out of the stream of negative peer pressure

A

and begin to surround yourself with those who are flying in the same direction. It is not enough, merely to stay stationary. One must have momentum in the right direction. Inertia is more easily overcome if those closest to you are travelling the same way you want to go.

NUMBER 3
ATTITUDE REVEALS INNER BELIEFS

Attitude may be intangible, nebulous and hard to define. Yet it is easy to spot. The state of being 'attitude neutral' is almost impossible. We send out 'vibes' or as Oddball describes them in one of my favourite films, <u>Kelly's Heroes</u>, 'waves'. Like the ocean, our innerself is constantly making waves which reach, via our attitude, far beyond our own physical body. Others can pick up on our attitude the moment we enter the room. Tone of voice, body language, our entire demeanour, are all the language of attitude.

A

Marshall Mcluhan coined the phrase, *'the medium is the message.'* The means of communication speaks louder than the words. Our attitude is far more important than our vocabulary. Bing Crosby was referring to this same truth when he sang, *'You don't need to know the language to say you are in love.'*

'I'm bored with you.' 'I like you.' 'I'm interested in what you have to say.' All these rarely need to be verbalised. Our attitude will do a powerful enough job by itself in getting these messages across, sometimes in the face of words that are saying the exact opposite. Thus the failure of angrily shouting, 'I love you,' or encouraging your spouse that you really care for her whilst your eyes are glued to the small screen.

Just the other day I was caught in a variation of the above. Heather and I were talking when suddenly she moved her head out of my line of sight. My eyes followed her but not without a delay. You see, I was listening but I was also thinking of something else. Heather said this was rude. I explained to her that I was preoccupied. Of course, I was listening

A

to her but I was doing other things as well - I was multi-tasking. I was considering many things! I am a complex person! Etc. etc. Yet after my hasty and, I might add, reasonably persuasive arguments, she merely again stated her point of view. 'You are being rude.' My words were saying one thing – my actions another. And now from a perspective of six months, I am slowly coming to the conclusion that she might be right! That crack you now see in my male ego is, I am told by competent authorities, only temporary!

To put it another way, attitude is rather like a smell . . . whether you happen to smell nice or nasty at this particular moment, is something that is already known by those who are in relatively close proximity. Our attitudes, in the same way, will quickly waft throughout our environment. Good healthy attitudes, I think, must smell like freshly ground coffee or baked bread, bacon and mushrooms frying or newly cut grass. The negative attitudes of life would be closer to open sewers, rotting food, or skunk-defence mechanisms. No wonder

A

self-defeating attitudes repel much of what we desire to see in our lives.

I have also observed just as someone who has B.O. seems unaware of it, so those with poor attitudes blame everything else and act as if they were oblivious to the real cause of the problem. The answer is, of course, not to get the air freshener out and mask or cover the problem, but to go the root of it, to take the shower, to wash the bin or throw out the cheese.

Attitude does not just reveal our emotional health, but affects our physical health as well. The local hospital at Moruya on the New South Wales far south coast, has recently opened a brightly decorated laughter room because the staff are so convinced that a patient's attitude affects their well-being. The evidence is continuing to grow that our psychological state has an important influence on our physical well-being, by helping to prevent diseases or affect recovery. Even something as serious as cardiovascular disease is more likely to be survived if the patient has a positive frame of mind. *'People who respond to pain in a catastrophic way, who repeatedly say, "I*

A

*can't go on. I can't manage," they are
the ones who don't manage.'* [3]

NUMBER 4
ATTITUDE ATTRACTS PEOPLE JUST LIKE US

We don't get the friends we want in life. We get the friends we are. We attract others or repel them not by our looks but by our attitudes. The negative gossip traders will quickly discover others just like them, and their constant attitude of pessimism will ensure that they never come into contact with people-loving, people-believing optimists.

I have noticed after being involved with various staffs and companies over the years that probably the greatest asset a manager can have is the ability to get along with people. Good people skills are by and large a product of attitude. The tragedy is that people with a lousy attitude don't realise that's what the problem is. They will blame the workplace as being unfair, peer employees who have sweet-talked the boss or they will simply put

A

their lack of promotion down to nepotism, favouritism, glass ceilings or prejudice. In short, the character flaws and personal problems of everybody else. Yet many times the reason they have not got to the place they thought they should have has nothing to do with the bias of others or their own lack of ability, rather it has everything to do with attitude. Skill levels can often be enhanced, but unfortunately an employee with a bad attitude usually refuses to believe that such an intangible can be so important and therefore rarely undergoes personal transformation.

Once we realise that the majority of our problems has to do with our own attitude rather than anything else, the quicker we will be on our way to successfully working with others and getting the best out of them. Our attitudes affect the people around us. Bad attitudes do not need to be introduced. Everyone around them recognises their presence . . . the 'vibes' are unmistakable. Yet the healthy attitude reveals itself quickly as well, winning over all within its reach. It is amazing to realise how much difference the tone of voice, the smile, the

A

handshake, can make. Such little things yet so impactful.

John Maxwell quotes one company's survey on why customers quit a certain retail franchise. The results were startling:

■ 1% because of death

■ 5% had developed other friendships

■ 3% had moved

■ 9% the price was what put them off

■ 14% was product dissatisfaction

■ But a massive 68% of customers who had quit shopping in this particular retail outlet had done so because of the indifference of an employee.

The attitude of a waiter or a shop assistant has a greater impact on the bottom line than almost any other single factor.

This type of attitude diminishes everybody around it whilst its opposite – the positive, go-the-extra-mile,

A

enthusiastic attitude - replenishes the lives within its range regardless of how fleeting the contact.

NUMBER 5
ATTITUDE AFFECTS REALITY

Attitude is not only about interpreting what is happening, a sort of 'feel-good' hype up which anaesthetises the pain of reality. No, attitude has the ability to actually change our worlds. Attitude is not only an internal disposition but it interacts with society, with emotional responses and practical doing. In fact the term attitude is often defined by psychologists in a far broader way than many of us would have in mind when we use the word.

Attitude covers three areas:

∎   Affection

∎   Cognition

∎   Behaviour

A

Affection could be defined as our evaluation of, liking or emotional response to people, concepts or objects.

Cognition has more to do with our beliefs and knowledge about these things.

Whereas behaviour is the way we actually act towards the person, the concept or the object.

My belief about whether or not a rainy day is a good day does not, of course, change the fact that it is raining. Yet my belief will lead to certain emotional responses and behaviours which will, in real terms, make a difference in how I live today. My interaction with people, my decisions as to what to do and what not to do, and my general demeanour throughout the day will all make a real difference to my life.

Indeed, success in life is all about these three areas:

■ what we believe,

■ how we emotionally respond, and

■ how we react.

Zig Ziglar tells a great story which illustrates this point in his best selling book, <u>See You At the Top</u>.[4] He was invited to speak at a real estate conference in Detroit in the midst of an automaker's strike. The strike was paralysing the local economy and was affecting a large proportion of the population. During the evening meal, prior to his speech he engaged in conversation with the people at the head table. Turning first to a gentleman on his right, he asked the question, 'How's business?' To which the response came back, 'Well, you know about the strike.' Ziglar nodded. 'Well, business couldn't be worse. People are insecure. Money is scarce. Long term security is threatened. We haven't sold a listing for months. If circumstances don't change we will be closing up shop in the not too distant future.' Ziglar was finally able to get out of this highly negative and depressing conversation and he turned his attention to the woman seated on his left and asked the same question. 'How's business?' Now understand, this was a real estate convention. They were both in the same business, in the same town, persevering under the same circumstances.

A

This lady replied to the question initially in the same way as the other gentleman. 'Well, you know there is a strike on at the moment.' Ziglar inwardly groaned. 'So, business could not be better. People have confidence that this is not going to last forever and besides that house prices are the lowest they have been for years. People have also got time on their hands. They will come out, look over several properties and go over them inch by inch from the attic to the cellar. We are selling tons of listings and if the strike goes on much longer I'm probably going to be able to retire!'

This is a classic case of attitude affecting reality. Now the strike was continuing regardless of the attitudes of the real estate agents but their attitudes affected their success or failure. I can almost picture how the conversations would go with prospective homebuyers from the two agents involved. The first by his very demeanour, tone of voice and negative disposition would very quickly put potential buyers off by giving them a sense of feeling foolish that they were buying at this time. Whereas the other agent was enthusing over their wisdom and their willingness to grab the wonderful opportunity that this set of circumstances had put before them.

Success in life, then, is not just about ability or knowledge, but about this so often overlooked ingredient of achievement. Increasingly people are beginning to realise that they must give more attention to this forgotten theme. Many employment programmes, that have been heavily competence based, are now beginning to make a shift in their emphasis of attitude. They are realising that what will gain the eye of the employer is not so much typing speed, or marks in exams, but the firm hand shake, the pleasant smile, the 'can-do' frame of mind. I only hope that one day the labour laws will catch up with truth in this regard. Today, in Australia, it is very difficult to fire anybody because of attitude, mainly because a bad attitude is hard to measure. The job may be being accomplished adequately but the negative waves and the passive resistance that poor attitudes in the workplace create are a greater threat to profitability than almost anything else. Yet unfortunately to act compassionately, yet clearly, with adequate due process on

A

the grounds of negative employee attitude is to face unfair dismissal complaints which will, in all probability, be upheld in court. It seems at present, that as long as you turn up at the required hours and do the minimum required, you have nothing to fear.

Successful companies, champion organisations, winning sports teams, or Amazing Achievers are never made of this kind of stuff. They are always looking for different ways to fire up their attitudes, to be more positive and enthusiastic, to view obstacles as opportunities and to serve everyone around them with joy. To change one's attitude is to change one's life. Regardless of who you are or what you do, having your attitude rethought and reengineered will always move you forward in the direction of your dreams, aspirations and hopes.

If you're going to do it, you might as well do it with attitude.

A

A

CHAPTER 3

WHERE DID THAT COME FROM?

'HOW ATTITUDE SPREADS'

If attitude is such a vital component in the cocktail of life how does one cultivate the power of positive attitude and discard the unwanted baggage of the self-defeating ones? If you lived in France and could only speak English, life would become reasonably frustrating. Trying to get your point across could never be assumed and unless you happened to be in a part of the country where everyone was bi-lingual you would soon resort to learning the language as quickly as you

A

could. There is nothing like ordering rognons de veau at a restaurant, expecting veal, only to find veal kidneys turn up on the plate. Personally speaking, as a result of such experiences, the French words for most animal organs are indelibly etched on my brain!

Attitude is very much like a language. To live with attitudes that repel success, disempower workmates and cause people to avoid you, is like living in a world where you are speaking the wrong kind of language. There needs to be a change. One must forget about the old and begin to learn the new.

While we will spend time later in this book identifying specific attitudes and discussing how to cultivate and sustain them throughout a lifetime. It would be helpful here to look at some general principles on how attitudes are acquired and developed.

A

ATTITUDES ARE CONTAGIOUS

Probably the primary way anybody picks up an attitude is by doing exactly that, picking it up.

Just hang around someone who is pessimistic and it begins to rub off on you. Before long you too are blaming the politicians, the interest rates, the corporate structure or the car for all of life's little frustrations. The same, of course, is true for attitudes on the positive side of the ledger.

Several months ago I happened to be in Melbourne on a Friday night. I noticed the MCG lights blazing away. For those who do not live in Australia the MCG is short for the Melbourne Cricket Ground, and is Australia's leading temple to the predominant religion, sport. I had never visited this esteemed arena so decided I would catch part of the evening's action. The game was Australian football and the teams were Richmond against the West Coast Eagles. Living on the West Coast I have become, by geographical necessity, and pastoral considerations (I think I

A

would be thrown out of our church if I confessed the sin of following any other football team!) a West Coast Eagles supporter. Yet, as chance would have it, I sat down amidst 50–60 thousand Richmond supporters. There I was looking very plain and drab amidst a sea of gold and black. I decided to take a low profile and was soon enjoying conversation with the ebullient spectators on either side of me. Slowly as the game proceeded I began to catch some of their enthusiasm. You feel like a right idiot not standing and cheering when the referee makes, to my mind, an obviously wrong decision. Yet, slowly their spirit began to infect me. I began to get excited when their team was doing well. I am not sure exactly why but it seems a pity to be in the midst of a party and not enjoy the festivities. It was not long before I too was a Richmond supporter.

For one evening, at least, I caught their attitude. (I should add, however, that it evaporated as soon as I got off the plane in Perth.) We pick up our attitudes, learn our accents from the people we spend our time with. This can, of course, work for

A

us or against us and brings to light several considerations.

Inoculate Against Bad Attitudes

If it is true that we can easily pick up the attitudes of those around us, then it makes sense to distance ourselves from the wrong kind of influence. There comes a time when who we are and our attitudes towards life are so well established that we would not be adversely affected by contrary pressure. Yet, in the initial stages it is wise not to hang around with attitudes that will diminish our lifestyle, impede our happiness, destroy our self-esteem or dissolve our destiny.

Sometimes this can prove painful. We value friendship; we want to run with the same crowd. My point is, however, that if you are not happy with where the crowd is running a choice needs to be made. You cannot run with your crowd and end up at a different destination.

Life has its phases. We are all on a journey. Sometimes we are privileged

A

enough to have people in our life who will journey with us for the entire distance. They share our values, commitment and see personal growth as a necessity. Yet there will be many others, who for a whole variety of reasons will not be as involved with us as they once were.

I have friends who were a lot closer to me ten years ago than they are today. When I went through my cynical stage I had many that would laugh at my jokes and join me as we criticised the game from the spectator stands. Yet, now I have moved on and the jokes aren't funny any more. I find life and fulfilment in trying to get involved and make a difference on the field. Unfortunately some of my friends are still in the stands and so by definition, although there has been no falling out, we are not as close. I know that if I allowed their attitude to permeate my life I could not be effective in doing what I sense I am meant to do.

Let me be quite clear, I am not advocating disloyalty to friends. All I am saying is that we must not allow ourselves, under the guise of 'mateship' (a great Australian value) to limit our growth, beliefs and

A

behaviour to that which will be accepted by our friends. There comes a time when we must grow up and run the race to which we are called, and hope that others will stay with us. If they choose not to, then run on we must.

This is all about who we allow to speak into our lives, who will be the ones we follow, whose attitudes we will seek to inculcate into our hearts and minds.

HANG AROUND HEALTHY ATTITUDES

If you want to learn how to sell real estate, don't spend your time with someone who has tried it and failed. If you want to learn about entrepreneurship in the free market, then maybe North Korea's business college would not be the most helpful. If your intent is growing roses, don't head for Antarctica! Successful attitude cultivation has a lot to do with being in the right environment and, as we have already mentioned, getting out of the wrong environment. One has to go, so to speak, where the gold is.

A

When seen in this light, who we spend our time with, the kind of books we read or videos we watch, begin to take on a more significant dimension. <u>Coral Island</u> is to be preferred to <u>Lord of the Flies</u> or preferably they are to be read together and the differences debated. Forrest Gump will prove more beneficial than Freddy Kruger, and the life modelled on the values of Mother Theresa, will produce fulfilment and significance far more than the life based on the values of Madonna. We all need heroes but the selection process is vital.

We must find a place where values, beliefs and attitudes are deposited, a place where people are made to think about the important things. A place where the big questions are asked and flabby thinking, frothy emotionalism or frivolous prejudice are banned. Where debate is encouraged without dissension, where individuality is encouraged, and the tendency to clone or conform for conformity's sake is worked against. Where truth is more important than popularity and authenticity prized over authoritarianism. A place where individual responsibility gets more airtime than individual rights and the

A

needs of the community are treated with great respect. In short, a place where morality, integrity and veracity are not gauged by the subjective opinion of the individual or the peer group pressure of the mass, but by that which is objective and other worldly. By those things that humanity over the bulk of its history, has highly respected.

For some this kind of environment can be created in the family, for others in their business or educational worlds, and for others the local church.

(I am, of course, a keen advocate for the local church because I find it one of the few places in contemporary western society which has a mandate to sow this kind of input into those who would call it their home.)

So then, it is necessary to hand around healthy attitudes and avoid the life-threatening ones. Every day we run into all sorts of people who carry all sorts of attitude. Some of them will make our day. Others, if we let them, will ruin it. We must keep on the look-out. Unfortunately

A

bad attitudes are in abundance and we therefore encounter them all too often.

Here is a brief guide to a few of the most common...

A Selection of Bad Attitudes

People are messed up, unhappy and depressed and their attitude to the world and everyone in it simply reveals their inner condition. So don't feel too guilty when you are on the receiving end of one of the following. You're probably not the one at fault, so don't take it too personally.

'The Can't Do' Attitude

This attitude is exemplified by the person who is an expert at thinking up reasons why something won't work rather than looking for ways it will. It is the overly intelligent fool who delights in throwing cold water on the creativity of others. Or the pedantic number cruncher who, in the middle of the brainstorming session, delights in sharing why we could never

A

afford it. They never act themselves, they merely point out why no one else can or should. John Naughton put it best when he said we must... *'Cast off the idiot questioner who is always questioning and never capable of answering, who sits with a sly grin, silent, plotting when to question, like a thief in a cave who publishes doubt and calls it knowledge, whose science is despair, whose pretence to knowledge is envy, whose whole science is to destroy the wisdom of ages to gratify ravenous envy.'*[5]

The other day, myself and a friend went to a small coffee shop in the middle of the afternoon to have a drink and talk over a few issues. When we entered the establishment we realised that at that time we were the only customers. Many of the tables had been prepared for dinner. (A few knives and forks and a couple of wine glasses.) As I like to spread, we asked to sit at a table that was larger than the rest. The waiter informed us that we couldn't sit there as it had been set for dinner and moved us to a small table devoid of items of cutlery. His attitude was very clear, 'I don't want to have to move a couple of knives and forks for you guys. After all

A

I work here and you're only the customer!'
Now sadly, in this particular case the
coffee was great and the food wonderful.
The owner, I am sure, thinks he has
covered all his bases and yet this one
waiter who has lost sight of the big picture
is probably damaging the profit margin
more than instant coffee would.

'AREN'T YOU STUPID' ATTITUDE

I experienced this one just yesterday.
Arriving to speak at a convention centre,
the parking attendant whose job it was to
direct cars to a certain part of the large
car park gave not only me but drivers in
front and behind that look which says, 'I
can't believe you people are so stupid in
that you do not know which part of this
car park you are meant to park in.' Well,
it was confusing, which is probably why
the place had employed her to help the
customers in the first place. The
arrangement of plastic cones merely
added to the confusion... Do we drive
around them, follow them to the right or
over them? This same look has been
developed by customs officials in strange

A

countries, wine waiters in expensive restaurants, accountants when you ask any form of question and, of course, politicians who hide behind a smoke screen of verbage and abstruse patronising jargon.

'THE MINIMUM REQUIRED' ATTITUDE

This one really gets my goat. It is frustrating because it is not in itself a bad attitude, it is simply the absence of all the good ones. It declares to everyone, 'I won't be mean and I won't be nice either. No snarling, no smiling. I will do just enough and never more than enough. I am not negative or positive. I won't fight a good idea, but I will never support one either.' It is the type of person who never goes the second mile. The waitress who tells you, you can't have eggs and chips because that combination is not on the menu and therefore to work out what it would cost is too much extra effort. These are the people who remain quiet when they should speak up, and ignore when they should lend a helping hand.

A

Their attitude is essentially selfish. They add nothing to their world, their company or their church. In fact, their net result is negative as they get on everyone's nerves by their frustrating lack of aliveness.

CHECK-OUT THESE ATTITUDES

On the other hand, I recently heard of a young man suffering with Downs Syndrome who worked at a checkout in a major supermarket. His job was to pack the bags of the customers as they came through his particular line. He had however, grabbed hold of this truth of attitude. He decided he would leave a signature on his work. He would do what he did better than everyone else around him. He began to spend his evenings looking for quotes from books and the Internet, and when he had found a suitable one, he would write it up, photocopy it, then cut each page up so he had hundreds of little slips of paper with the quote of the day written upon them. Then for the whole of the next working day he would put his 'Thought for the Day' into each bag he packed.

A

A couple of weeks went by and the store manager noticed that one checkout line had three times as many people as all the others. She quickly tried to organise some more checkout operators and began to direct customers to these new open lines but met, to her surprise, great resistance. 'No,' they protested, 'We want to get our thought for the day.' It didn't take long for that young man to become the store's most valuable employee. Whatever we do, attitude will make the difference.

I remember with fondness one such individual who made a difference in hundreds of lives a day without speaking to a soul.

He worked in my home city of Perth, as a children's crosswalk attendant. This elderly gentleman's job was to stand at a strategic crosswalk where three roads met and help children get across the road. Yet, what he did, he did with attitude. He would position himself on the central island and while waiting for groups of children would wave and smile at every car, from every direction. He used all his arms and legs, and would playfully wink to all and sundry. I can remember

A

choosing to drive to work via this particular intersection just so I would get a smile. Although this man was not a celebrity, never made the papers, and finally retired, he was known and loved by hundreds of people. In fact, I hardly ever talked about him without someone else in the group agreeing and nodding and saying that they drove that way as well. Who cares about a mild traffic jam when you are going to receive a little bit of attitude?

A

CHAPTER 4

FROM SMALL TO LARGE

'How Attitude Grows'

Every attitude that I have towards life, people, God, objects and concepts, I have as the small or large plant of what was once a tiny seed. A friend, relative or teacher may have deposited it, or I may have discovered it myself in my own reading and thinking. A freak occurrence, painful circumstance or abusive slur may have placed it within. Yet whether the seed grows and becomes part of who I am is very much based on the attention, nurture and protection I give it.

A

The words, 'The people of that race are always arrogant,' once heard can be planted and encouraged to grow, or just as easily discarded onto the rubbish heap upon which belongs all prejudice. Yet when the seed is first presented, many of us lack the understanding, sophistication or the overall wisdom to understand what is happening. We tend to allow our attitudes and our beliefs to slowly evolve without foresight or planning. When we realise what is going on, it has almost become a lost cause. The plant has taken over the pot and removal requires considerable energy and time.

One of the keys therefore, of cultivating healthy attitudes is to keep your eye out for the seeds... constantly planting or discarding. Every day they are dropped onto our life. If we do nothing, all sorts of things may spring up. Beautiful gardens need a good amount of work. Great lives don't just happen. Amazing attitudes are not arbitrary or accidental. They are planned, cared for, fertilised and watered and, I should hasten to add, their fruit is not enjoyed immediately. Yet given time, fruit will come. The life will be enriched or almost destroyed, depending upon the

A

harvest that has been allowed to grow from the soil.

The garden metaphor proves helpful on several fronts. It makes the point well that attitudes take time to develop and that instant transformation is to be discarded in preference to long term, systematic progress. All an attitude is, is a small seed. Given time we can often overlook this as we have a tendency, in our culture, to despise the small, and get excited about the grand.

SMALL IS MORE THAN JUST BEAUTIFUL

The movie Titanic is a metaphor of our times in many different ways. The top deck of civilisation is beginning to tilt yet we continue with our cocktails and our card games, oblivious to our impending doom. Those who work below deck, away from the myopia of self-absorption, see the real story. Yet Titanic is also an illustration of how we are often enamoured with the large and despise the small. We love the biggest and the best. We look down our noses at what we

A

perceive to be the insignificant small things.

The main news in Perth over the last week was the visit of the supermodel, Elle McPherson. She shouldn't have been, of course, because she wasn't. The fastest or most beautiful are not the ones creating history. The Roman Empire grabbed the headlines of its day but there was an insignificant group of disciples in a small room somewhere in Jerusalem in AD 30 who were the real story of their time.

As a growing boy, one of my favourite books was the <u>Guinness Book of Records</u>, and its popularity simply shows that I am not alone in marvelling at that which pushes the limits. I have climbed the Empire State Building, the World Trade Centre in New York, as well as Sears Tower in Chicago. (Although when I say climbed, I mean I climbed into the elevator and then out of it again!) I visited these buildings like so many other millions, not only for the view, but to experience the tallest and then to brag about it afterwards. The myth of big is not that big is somehow bad but that it can delude us either into thinking that big

A

is better or impress us to the point that the process is lost and only the event, the destination, the final product is important. Life, however, is all about process. First you have to start out small and then that which is small must be given the chance to grow.

Our attitudes are like seeds. The point of the simile is that seeds are incredibly small and yet have the potential of birthing large things. Yet for this to happen, there must be labour, diligence and patience - characteristics that are often spurned in today's world. The quality of vision, for example, is able to see not only the seed but also its potential. Vision would have us consider and then invest in the young Bill Gates as he sat in his garage wanting a few thousand to start a company. Those who are enamoured by the large would dismiss him as a young nerd.

THE POWER OF MULTIPLICATION

In the New Testament, Jesus describes the entire Kingdom of God as a seed. As

A

is evidenced by the context, and by the history of the early church, what he had in mind was the explosive power of multiplication. That within a seed are all the necessary ingredients, the unrealised potential, the things that are necessary to grow into that which is very large. We ourselves are good examples of this. The multiplying effect of the sperm meeting the egg results in fully adult human beings 20 years later. Yet all the information for this to occur was contained within the very first cell.

This principle of multiplication is found throughout the world. If we are continually focused on the large, we will underestimate the power of the small. Saving a $1.00 a day is not really worthwhile, except when you realise over a working life, invested at 10% compounding annually, the amount will grow to $215,000. $5.00 a day will grow to well over $1 million.

To reach our world with any message worth communicating, be it the evangelist or the educator, the job becomes easier and effective if we start small and go slow. The evangelist who can reach 10,000 a

A

day over 30 years will communicate to 117 million people. Yet if the same individual spent one year in communicating and reproducing himself in one other, and the following year the two of them both communicated in order to reproduce themselves again. Over the same 30 year period, this pattern continuing, 7 billion would be reached. The previously impressive 117 million, of the former strategy, is only 1.4% of the latter.

I remember as a teenager having a hypothetical posed to me in regard to multiplication and earnings. Just imagine if a prospective employer came to you and asked you to work for a month for them and then gave you some payment options. You could either receive your earnings in the form of $10,000 per day or 1 cent the first day, 2 cents the second day, 4 cents the third day, doubling until the end of the month. Which would you choose? The hasty often go for the $10,000 a day. After all at the end of the week you would have $70,000 in the bank. Whereas if you had chosen the other method you would have the grand sum of $1.27. Yet the wise realise that

A

multiplication, given time, is uncatchable. On the last day of the month the hasty employee would earn his $10,000, whereas the wise would earn $10,737,418.27. The total amount earned would be $21,485,323.23. It is interesting to note that the multiplying method only overtakes the daily amount earned on day 21 and overtakes the total amount earned in the first part of day 26.

This truth, of course, works not only in the positive but in the negative as well. Small problems can build into large ones. Divorces are often a result of little things that went untouched, unspoken about, unresolved for long periods of time. The Book of Proverbs compares the beginning of strife to a small crack in the bottom of a dam. Like the hole in the dyke, eventually a very small thing can destroy a very large thing. The size of the holes that sank Titanic are an adequate illustration of the danger of underestimating the small.

One's attitude, if minimalised, has the potential of scuttling the life, and if nurtured and developed has the capacity

A

to place its owner's hands on the dreams
and destiny of their heart.

A

SECTION II - SEVEN ATTITUDES

A

CHAPTER 5

RUNNING WITH THE HORSES

'THE ATTITUDE OF EXCELLENCE'

'A PERSON'S QUALITY OF LIFE IS A FOREMEASURE OF A PERSON'S COMMITMENT TO EXCELLENCE, REGARDLESS OF WHAT FIELD THEY MAY BE IN.'

VINCE LOMBARDI

I have just come home, after a day's writing, to a wife who is smiling wide, brimming over with confidence as she proudly points to her latest exam results; 100% . . . again! Heather is doing part-

A

time studies for a horticultural degree and is doing very well. The examiner's comments on the bottom of the page simply state, 'Excellent work. Outstanding.' For Heather, this is a first. When she was at school she never exerted herself and as a consequence had mediocre results. Never before has she done so well in an exam. The rest of the family are now destined for the next week or two to walk around genuflecting regularly and declaring, 'we are not worthy'!

Developing an excellent attitude, however, is not about getting 100%. It is about doing the best you can with what you have. It is a refusal to adopt a half-hearted, sloppy, 'near enough is good enough' perspective of life. To be honest, when I was in high school I rarely exerted myself more than was necessary. Passing was my goal, not excelling. Yet if this attitude is maintained throughout the years, it will cause irreparable harm and shackle the life in such a way that it will rarely rise above the average.

Excellence simply refuses to believe that near enough is good enough. This may be

A

true, of course, in some areas of life. Yet in these times of increasing precision and competition this kind of thinking is simply not acceptable. In fact, when we extrapolate the figures we can see that in many areas our world would be horrific if we accepted the notion that 99.9% was okay.

For example, if 99.9% was deemed to be our benchmark, then

- in Perth, Western Australia, 1,000 homes would be without power today.

- 30,000 Australians would have their tax documents lost this year.

- 1,000 babies would go to the wrong parents out of every million births.

- 15,000 defective tyres would be shipped all over our country.

- 1 Australian federal politician would be caught in a scandal every four years!

■ 300 planes would crash worldwide every day.

All right then, so at least one of these would be an improvement!

The kind of thinking that puts up with the shabby, sloppy, wishy-washy, mediocre and insipid, rings the death-knell on achievement, innovation and creativity every time.

John Gardiner puts it this way:

> *'A society that scorns excellence in plumbing because it is a humble activity and tolerates shoddiness in philosophy because it is an exalted activity will have neither good plumbing nor good philosophy. Neither its pipes nor its theories will hold water.'*

Excellence is always being willing to give it your best shot. To do what we do with all our might and to stubbornly refuse to take shortcuts that will lower quality or diminish effectiveness. TQM (Total Quality Management) is now simply considered to be common sense in the

A

marketplace, and must be adopted in our lives as well. Nothing less than a Total Quality Attitude will cause us to achieve to our potential.

WHAT EXCELLENCE IS NOT

The dictionary simply defines excellence as, *'surpassing merit, pre-eminence.'* Yet, probably the best way to work out what something is, is to see what it is not. This is certainly true with the concept of excellence.

Here are a couple of attitudes that are falsely called excellence by some and therefore tend to give this attitude a bad name.

NUMBER 1
NEUROTIC PERFECTIONISM

The inability to relax because there is a scrap of paper on the bathroom floor or a slight mistake in a class presentation; lying awake all night worrying because the spring rolls ran out at the 21st birthday

A

party, or a critical catch was dropped in the social game. These are all signs that perspective has been lost. The minor has become the major and the concept of being the best you can, has been drowned in an ocean of minutiae and pettiness.

Usually perfectionism of this kind only extends to the external and visible. The same diligence is not applied to matters of character and morality, marriage or child raising. It is nothing more than looking for self-worth and the appreciation of others, in all the wrong places. The issue here has ceased to be doing one's best because it is the right thing; it merely camouflages a sense of inferiority and low self-esteem. This difference of motivation is what separates excellence from perfectionism.

When things fail and mistakes happen, the perfectionist will take it all too personally and sink further into the mire of self-depreciation. Whereas the individual committed to excellence will learn from mistakes and get on with the job, secure in the knowledge that they gave it their best shot.

A

I might also add, that some resist the attitude of excellence and prefer mediocrity due to self-esteem problems as well. In this situation the individual feels like they do not deserve the best and if they gave it their all it wouldn't amount to a whole lot anyway, so why bother. After all, if I never really try, then the fantasy that if I really did, I'd be a champion, can never be tested. I remain a hero in my own mind, too scared of failure to ever attempt. Unsure of what my full potential is, I choose to do nothing. I then become, as a result, like sports cars that are never taken out of the garage for fear there might be an accident. To live so is to live retarded lives, where potential is unreached and dreams are unfulfilled.

As the car is designed to be driven, the plane to be flown, so the human has been designed for Amazing Achievements - to never attempt is to die quietly, years before the funeral.

A

NUMBER 2
SNOBBISH SOPHISTICATION

This attitude masquerades as excellence but feels like a put-down. Again, the difference here is obvious, once you go below the surface to the underlying motive. In trying to do my best to prove that I'm better than everyone else, I simply reveal my problem is self-esteem and pride. Excellence is not based upon the foundation of personal inadequacy or self-aggrandisement, but because the task, the job, the career, the marriage, the life itself, warrants our best.

In our church in Perth, we have a list of ten values on which we try to base everything we do. One of them enshrines this particular attitude of excellence with the simple sentence, *'Excellence honours God and inspires people.'* We believe that things should be done with our whole hearts because it is part of our worship. In the Old Testament the sacrifices that were made had to be from the best rather than from the worst of the flock because it follows logically that if there is a God, then he deserves our very best. It is our attitude that worships Him. Not only that,

A

but excellence inspires people. When something is done well, everyone involved in it rises to a new level. People love to be giving their time and effort to something that gleams with excellence.

One would think that the concept of a divine audience would make it easier for the theist to do things well. Unfortunately the track record of much of Christianity shows the opposite to be the case. Many Christians, unfortunately, reason that God is good and gracious, He looks at the heart and therefore if we are working for Him, He is not nearly as demanding as some secular company which has profit for the bottom line. Such logic is unbiblical, an excuse for laziness, an appalling loss of foresight and wisdom, and one of the major reasons many turn their back on the church. What is meant to be the light of the world has become both shabby and mediocre.

Top sports teams, innovative manufacturers and corporate entities will always strive for excellence. They realise it is one of the major keys to success. Every champion, regardless of their field, endeavours to be extraordinary, totally

A

committed, striving for the highest standards, operating at their peak potential. With this attitude they push themselves to new levels and discover new sources of strength that are untapped and unrealised by the restless, lukewarm and mediocre majority.

CHARACTERISTICS OF EXCELLENCE

NUMBER 1
SEEN IN THE DETAIL

> *'It's the little foxes that spoil the vine.'*[6]

Excellence is not as clearly seen in the big things as it is in the little things. Removing the little scuff on the shoe before the presentation, giving a little bit of extra thought to picking the appropriate word for the occasion, reprinting a brochure because the first time wasn't good enough, and letting your spouse know that you are going to be late by an

A

extra half-an-hour, when it would be easier not to worry about it.

Excellence is mindful that it is small leaks that sink big boats as the recent research into Titanic amply proved; the Space Shuttle exploded for want of a filter. Many of the world's tragedies have their cause in a minor fault. Bob Richards, the Olympic pole-vaulter, put it this way: *'You don't win unless you conquer the little flaws.'* Indeed, a cursory look at creation brings out the point that God is into detail. What would human beings be without nasal hair or dimples? What would this world be like without polychromatic Amazonian birds or 10,000 varieties of beetle? The intricacies of the microscopic world simply make this point more compelling. One would think that the closer we looked, the more fuzzy things would become; yet we have discovered a world within a world. Attention to detail is something that is found within the DNA of every living thing.

When the Statue of Liberty was refurbished and renovated at America's bicentennial it was reported that the top of the head had hair on it (Something not so encouraging to us bald folks!) What makes this remarkable is when the statue was created, the sculptor had no way of knowing that people would be able to fly and see that which is hidden by the height and by the crown. The attention to detail simply reveals the spirit of excellence in the creator.

Michelangelo's painting of the Sistine Chapel has the same hallmark. When he was asked why he was spending so much time in the dark corners where no one would be able to see, he is reported to have said, *'God will.'* That way of thinking has an air of greatness to it. What matters is not what people will see but how we live with ourselves after we have finished. Excellence is not about impressing other people; it is about doing it right because it is the right thing to do.

A

NUMBER 2
EXCELLENCE GOES THE SECOND MILE

In the celebrated Sermon on the Mount, Jesus spoke about the need to do more than is required if one is to win the admiration, favour and respect of those who would oppress. On the other hand, the legalists and Pharisees did only as much as was required. The average person works from nine to five but those who are excellent go beyond this. They put in extra effort, extra energy and therefore they are the most underpaid staff we have. Underpaid, not in the sense that they do not receive good remuneration but that they are continually doing more than what they are paid for. This, of course, ensures continued pay rises; something that the small-minded never seem to grasp.

Charles Schultz, the celebrated cartoonist responsible for Peanuts said, *'Just try to draw a good strip every day.'* His point was that many who desire to be cartoonists and are just beginning have a tendency to think they should save their best work until they are discovered. Schultz however, makes the point:

A

'You should start doing your great things right away. I think this is the secret in any sort of performing art. Not trying to save yourself for the great day when you become famous, but just do the best you can each day.'

The attitude of holding oneself back rather than committing to excellence actually robs the individual of their future. For it is in doing one's best work before there is prominence that one gets noticed. I have had employees on my staff, hoping for a promotion to be head of their department, doing just enough to get the job done, but holding onto their best ideas and best work in the fear that whoever is leading that area would gain the credit. This kind of paranoia not only robs the organisation but robs the individual as well. In refusing to give they will never receive. Through selfishness and fear, excellence is delayed. Yet true excellence can never be delayed and will simply evaporate from the life that tries to hide it in these ways.

The rewards in life only come after the effort is expended. Therefore, excellence should be an obvious truth. We should all

A

be saying, 'Of course, if I want to live an abundant life in every area, I must put in more than is expected and do it before I see the benefits accrue.' With this kind of thinking the marriage, the family, our spirituality, character, business, indeed everything we put our hands to, will begin to grow and flourish.

The second mile, you see, is never crowded. Or as Zig Ziglar puts it, *'There is plenty of room at the top.'*

NUMBER 3
EXCELLENCE IS BEING WILLING TO GO TO THE NEXT LEVEL

'If you have run with the footmen and they have tired you out, how can you compete with the horses?'[7]

The attitude of excellence would encourage us to run with the horses rather than shuffle with the crowd, to soar with the eagles instead of cackling with the hens, to purr with the Porsches rather than

A

spluttering with the Skodas! The excellent attitude is always looking for new heights, new levels and new challenges. Excellence enabled Bannister to break the four-minute mile; Hillary to climb Everest; Suzie Maroney to swim between Cuba and America.

New breakthroughs in science, technology or even customer service are usually driven by this attitude of excellence. I was talking to a friend the other day who had recently flown on Virgin Airlines Business Class. He was excited, well actually he was a bit of a pain as he went on and on about how wonderful it was. For those of us who fly mainly in Economy it wasn't at all nice to hear what I'm missing out on. First of all, he was picked up from his hotel in a Range Rover that took him directly to the airport and through customs. He didn't even have to get out of the car. The driver took his passport and tickets in, and then came back having checked him through. He was then taken to the special lounge – not just a regular private lounge, but one complete with its own complimentary restaurant and putting green! The flight itself continued to surprise, with an onboard

A

physiotherapist, manicurist and masseur.
I tell the story for two reasons:

■ First, I think it is an excellent example of taking, in this case Business Class hospitality, to a whole new level; to be the best one can be, to go the second mile, to put in that extra effort and stun the customer. Tom Peters would call it the *'Wow factor'*.

■ The second reason is the hope that any staff, management, or best of all the CEO of Virgin Airlines happens at any time in their life to read this particular volume. I am hoping that maybe ten years hence, I'll receive an upgrade certificate on a trans-Atlantic flight! Now that would be an excellent thing for Richard Branson to do!

EXCELLENCE — AN ATTITUDE UNDER THREAT

Probably of all the attitudes we are looking at in this volume, the attitude of excellence is the most endangered. If it

A

were a house, the local council would be preserving it. If it were an animal, Greenpeace would be campaigning on behalf of it. Yet, because it's just an attitude, no one seems to notice its demise. Indeed if anything, the majority hasten its extinction.

Those who choose to go the extra mile, find the pathway relatively untrod. There are several reasons for this. Primary amongst them is the fact that society by and large is prejudiced against excellence. Excelling shows up mediocrity for what it really is. Lifting the bar a few more inches increases the pressure on everybody else.

Those who are happy to just get by, who are committed to mediocrity rather than significance, resent this sense of being shown up for what they really are. It's a little bit like the crabs trying to climb out of the basket. The moment one moves up the side the others grab hold of it and pull it down again. In the Australian culture, this phenomenon is called the Tall Poppy Syndrome. One would think that we would be inspired to grow or delight in the shade offered by those around us who

A

have gone to the next level. Yet, rarely is this the response of society to those who move ahead of the pack. We all want heroes but we also want to believe that they were just lucky. If they fall, so be it, and we will enjoy reading about their foibles and frailty in the next edition of our favourite magazine.

Maybe another reason why excellence is not more widespread is that the majority of us are rarely challenged or led in this direction. We are told not to dream too big or work too hard. In an age where the individual is primary, there seems little to drive us beyond average. It has been my observation that those who do excel in life tend to have other people in mind. They are trying their best not just for themselves, but because they are gripped by some greater goal.

You have to have a dream, a lofty ideal, a reason bigger than yourself to get up in the morning and to give it your best shot. As Tom Peters said, *'A passion for excellence means thinking big and starting small. Excellence happens when high ideals and intense pragmatism meet.'* Without such a faith in the future we lack

A

the power to maintain peak performance in the present. The goal becomes both the target and fuel, and the larger the goal the more we are inspired to do it well.

I like what Winston Churchill once said, *'If you're doing big things, you attract big people. If you're doing little things, you attract little people. Little people usually cause trouble.'*

Pettiness, bureaucracy and ultraconservatism constantly wage their war against innovation, leadership and excellence. The soldiers of Israel were the ones who laughed at, discouraged and then criticised David for taking on Goliath. He showed up their lack of faith and vision. For them, Goliath was too big to hit, for David he was too big to miss.

So, then, excellence is a journey. It is an attitude that continually looks to improve. As my Greek teacher used to say, 'It's the daily dose that does it.' An excellent attitude looks at the task, the marriage, the life, and continues to make small, incremental changes. As Pat Riley has said, *'Excellence is the gradual result of always striving to do better.'*

A

The average begins when we cease to explore new territory, learn new facts or do new things. The excellent are willing to take risks and try new challenges. The question, 'When was the last time you did something for the first time?' is always answered with a smile and a reference to a recently completed activity or event.

This is all because being excellent is not a stagnant thing. It is either growing or diminishing. Excellence must continue to increase. If it does not, it is no longer excellent. It will quickly become status quo. The reason that many of the companies listed in Tom Peters' study detailed in his book, <u>In Search of Excellence</u>, had failed a decade down the track was because they saw excellence as a destination. When Peters wrote about them, they thought they had arrived, so they pulled the vehicle over and set up for a picnic, not realising that as they did so, excellence was already a mile down the road.

A

A

CHAPTER 6

WHY NORMAN WAS RIGHT

'THE ATTITUDE OF CONFIDENCE'

There has probably been more written about this particular attitude than any other. Norman Vincent Peale became known the world over because of his landmark book on developing a positive, mental attitude. Indeed the term has produced an entire industry, while in some circles the concept has become more of a pejorative. This is unfortunate. Some have diminished it to simply superficial hype or cosmetic camouflaging, a sort of 'grin and bear it', singing: 'Always look

A

on the bright side of life,' as we are nailed to our respective crosses. The Monty Python team and others have rightly parodied such an attitude.

Yet, let's not throw the baby out with the bathwater. Surely Peale and the many others who have written along this line, did not have in mind such extremes. The cynical find it easy to knock down this particular straw man without realising that there is far more than straw within the concept of developing a faith-filled, confident view of life. For this reason, I have used the word confidence, rather than optimism or positivity. The former has a sense of heart to it. The latter have been reduced, at their best, to emotionalism and, at their worst, pretence.

THE PROBLEM IS THE CONTEXT

This attitude of confidence or faith is often only seen within the context of a problem. The Promised Land is rarely the peaceful land. It is only when obstacles abound or when war looms that the determination and strength of positive expectation are

A

seen. Indeed, without its inner fortitude we are left with only despair and negativity, which drain us of energy and have us fleeing before the battle heats up.

An attitude of confidence is all about how we deal with problems, not a false expectation that there will be none. Problems and pain are part of life and things aren't wrong just because things are wrong. This has been axiomatic throughout most of human history. It is only in modern times, thanks to the pervasiveness of technology, that we have begun to consider that life is meant to be Utopia. We want pain minimisation and climate-controlled environments. We worship comfort and convenience and get upset over the minor irritations of life - 'It's not fair. It shouldn't be this way.' We quickly look for someone to blame, to point the finger at, or to take to court.

Just the other day, when staying in a motel, I was horrified to realise that the television set did not have a remote. This meant that I had to get out of bed every time I wanted to change a channel. How difficult my life had become! I allowed this little frustration to almost become

A

the overwhelming reality of my life that particular evening.

We have slowly been conditioned to think that growth should come without groaning, happiness without heartbreak, potential without pain, discipleship without discipline. We want the benefits without the bills and success without sacrifice. We want deliverance without disturbance and reward without responsibility. We want the blessing; we don't want the blisters. In short, we want to play but we don't want to pay. We revel in resurrection yet we want to arrive there by avoiding Gethsemane much less the cross!

The attitude of confidence realises, however, that there will be walled cities and giants, conflicts and challenges. Yet the only way to deal with such *'slings and arrows of outrageous fortune'* is to look them in the eye and address them with a sense of hope in our voice whilst all the time expecting victory.

I have a poster on our Boardroom wall that was used to inspire this kind of confidence in World War II England. It

A

is simply a line drawing of Churchill, eyes ahead, finger pointing, with the words, 'Deserve Victory'. Great things in life don't just happen, their needs to be a fight and only those who are prepared for the battle at its worst, whilst believing in the best, have the necessary arsenal to see it through.

IT ALL COMES FROM THE HEART

One of the key truths of ancient wisdom comes from the Book of Proverbs where King Solomon declares, *'Guard your heart with all diligence for from it flow the forces of life.'* [7]

The reason many think of attitude as a lightweight subject is because they see it as a sham. You feel like frowning but smile. You want to shout out your frustrations and failures but you mouth platitudes instead. This concept is adopted by glitzy evangelists and low-integrity sales organisations the world over. As a result the high moral ground has been left to the doom sayers and gloom merchants. Despair has been exalted to be the

A

philosophical choice of our postmodern youth, and the suicide rate and drug overdose statistics are merely a barometer of its popularity.

In the 60's people took LSD to discover what life was about. At the changing of the millennia the reasons have far more to do with escaping. When there is nothing to live for, why live at all? If hope is just hype then black melancholy has no champions to face. The dragon has won and Sir Lancelot is dead. We, along with John Lennon, imagined there was no heaven but in so doing we discovered we were living in hell, like 'the nothing' in the Never Ending Story. Our disintegration is accelerating.

Faith and hope, however, are not words that should be relegated to some theological backwater. They have the power, when unleashed in our lives, to transform. To start, nothing less than a revolution. Vaclav Havel armed with such a philosophy of hope has brought a new-found purpose and meaning to his home country of Czechoslovakia. Here within my own country of Australia we are seeing something of a spiritual revival amongst

A

the Buster Generation as a new kind of hope takes hold.

We have become civilised and cultured, balancing nuclear deterrents and nuclear freedom, yet we cannot master our own misery. We have everything, yet we have nothing. Multiple accessories, miniaturisation and medical marvels matter little when there is a dark void within. Angst, anxiety, disillusionment and depression walk our streets in every increasing numbers, and it is only when a deeper, more thoughtful kind of hope wins our hearts and minds that these barbarians of the soul will be vanquished.

It would be easy here to draw up a list of steps to positive living . . . but that all sounds too boring! So let us approach the subject from the other end. In a positive attempt to delineate negatively the impact of positive negativism!

THREE KEYS TO NEGATIVITY

A

NUMBER 1
ONLY HAVE EYES FOR THE PROBLEM

Negativity is all about what you see. The glass is half-empty. The sky is partly cloudy. There is so much I haven't got. The wrinkles are increasing whilst my hair is diminishing.

Opportunities are not so much ignored, as they are simply not spotted. The concentration is on what is wrong, therefore the dreams of what could be are fuzzy and out of focus. Here worry and gossip become the two greatest allies of the negative person. They allow the individual to focus only on the problem. To think about it all the time whilst in the process gaining a misguided sense of personal uniqueness as we consider how unfortunate we are. In this way, even after the crisis is over, it will never be forgotten. And when something else goes wrong, the phrase, 'it's happening to me again' flows sweetly and automatically from the lips.

A

NUMBER 2
TURN MOLEHILLS INTO MOUNTAINS

Negativity not only constantly views the problem but exaggerates it as well. When Moses was attempting to lead the children of Israel into the Promised Land, they became highly negative, to the point when reality took second place to perception. *'We became like grasshoppers in our own sight and so were we in their sight.'*[9]

It's a little bit like the four Yorkshiremen in that great old Monty Python skit where each is trying to outdo the others on how bad things were 'forty-year-ago'. The skit culminates with the lines:

> *'Well, we used to get up in the morning, half-past ten at night, half an hour before we went to bed, eat a lump of freezing cold poison, go work down mill twenty-eight hours a day and pay the owners to let us work there, and when we got home our dads would murder us in cold blood and dance about on our grave singing Hallelujah . . . And you try telling*

A

*that to the young people of today
and they won't believe you!'* [10]

Every now and then a sufferer of
theological negativity (I think the Bible
referred to these people as Pharisees)
comes up to me in the church. Their
complaint may have some merit but what
annoys me the most is when I hear the
refrain, 'Everybody is saying this.' If one
is to enquire as to who the 'everybody'
is, we might discover there are three or
four people out of a couple of thousand
who feel the same way. I was amused
when George Negus, the well-known
Australian reporter, tried this ploy on
Margaret Thatcher some years ago. He
was in Number Ten Downing Street, doing
an in-depth interview and made the
statement, 'When we're on the street
people will often come up to us and say
that Margaret Thatcher is not so much
stubborn as she is pig-headed. How do
you respond to that?'

To which Mrs Thatcher replied, 'Who has
said this to you?'

'Well, people on the streets,' replied
Negus.

A

Pushing again, Mrs Thatcher asked, 'Who are these people? How many of them? Do you have their names?'

George spluttered and then shut up. He was, of course, inventing and exaggerating, and when called to account for this was left with nothing but embarrassment.

Negativity, when so confronted, often discovers that the facts, upon which it was based, dissolve. This is because negativity is more of an interpretation, a slant, a spin, than it is about tangible, realistic objectivity.

NUMBER 3
FORM A TEAM

It is an interesting phenomenon, how like attitudes attract others of the same species. If you want to find resentful people, start being resentful. Begin to fake authenticity and you will discover plastic people wherever you go. In the same way, when you start being negative you will find many comrades in arms. I am not sure how it works but there is definitely some form of attitude magnetism.

This is beneficial in several different ways.

First of all, as we have already mentioned, it now enables you to use that wonderful line, 'everybody is saying...'. What you mean by this, of course, is that everybody you spend time with is saying this. Mainly because they like what you are saying and agree with you. Those who don't quietly disappear from view.

Secondly, a group of pessimists can be exponentially more negative than a lone one could ever be. This is why a group of people being cynical will cancel out a group of people being positive. Providing numbers are roughly equal, nothing will get done. It is upon this truth that most of western democracy has its foundation!

A

CHAPTER 7

HUMDRUM IS HO-HUM

'THE ATTITUDE OF ENTHUSIASM'

The story is told of a small boy who had just discovered the game of baseball. He had spent most of the week practising and could hardly wait to show his father his new-found skills. With boundless enthusiasm he grabbed his dad's hand the moment he arrived home from work, dragged him to the back lawn and said, 'Dad, watch me!' Throwing the baseball up in the air, he swung the bat and missed the ball by quite a large margin. He repeated this three times, each time failing to connect or even get close to getting a hit. He then turned and looked at his father, face beaming, 'Well,' he said, 'What do you think? Aren't I a great pitcher?!'

Enthusiasm is like that. It sees things from a different perspective. It takes the humdrum of every day existence and injects it with vitality and vibe. Without it, life can be pretty dreary. With it, the eyes shine at the dawning of each new morn.

Enthusiasm has this ability to make the ordinary wonderful. This again re-emphasises my major thesis; that attitude is the making or the breaking of each passing moment. When someone, not acquainted with this truth, meets an enthusiast, he or she is likely to postulate as to why this person is bubbling over with such ebullience. 'Something good has probably happened to them,' or 'their ship has come in', 'their job pays well' or 'their marriage must be wonderful.' Yet to judge so is to misjudge. For real enthusiasm is always character-based and never context-driven.

Now, I am not at all saying that our external world has no effect upon our demeanour. Certainly to have the woman you love say, 'I do', or to experience the pain of a close friend's betrayal, has a bearing on our emotions and our moods. Our happiness can go up or down based on the 'happenings' that we experience. Yet, genuine enthusiasm finds its roots spring from within the life rather than from the environment. Skin-deep excitement is something altogether different. Unfortunately many observe this poor relation and jump to the conclusion that this is what enthusiasm is all about, a surface hype; something that is felt at the political rally, sales meeting or the sports game, something which fades quickly after the event; a feeling that can be created artificially but is fleeting at best.

I well remember my first conscious experience of this phenomenon. Our family had moved to America to study in preparation for Christian ministry. My younger sister and brother attended the local primary and secondary schools. In dropping them off to school one morning, I noticed a large crowd of students

A

gathering together in the front of the school making an incredible amount of noise. 'There must be a fight,' I mused. For in New Zealand schools this was the only reason why students would form such a huddle. Penny, my sister, quickly informed me that this was a 'pep-rally', a kind of adolescent, motivational frenzy. The American culture, by and large, is addicted to this kind of buzz. We see it in the cheerleaders, at every sporting event, to the vociferous interjections of agreement and approval I get whenever I speak in that wonderful land!

Now, don't get me wrong, I am certainly not against this sort of thing. Although I am from conservative British stock and used to joke about such antics with lines like, 'It's an empty drum that makes the most noise,' and 'quiet waters run deep,' I realise now that there is nothing wrong with a little bit more excitement in the air. And speaking purely as a pastor, I think one of the major problems with many of our churches is that they are too intense, too serious and too restrained. Faith should not just cause the heart to delight and the mind to think, but the mouth to shout and the body to dance. I

A

am however, making the point that such excitement is not enthusiasm because its fundamental nature relies on encouragement and persuasion from without rather than contemplation and vision from within.

LAWN BOWLS CAN BE GRIPPING!

Here in Australia, we have a sports commentator named Darryl Eastlake. Darryl is one of those bubbly kind of guys, who no matter who he is with or what he is talking about, exudes a passion beyond the ordinary. His sports commentary (although I expect it gets on some people's nerves) is second to none. He doesn't need the game or the event to be really happening, he just gets behind the microphone, and just happens himself!

Recently Darryl was commentating at the Commonwealth Games where around 120 countries, which make up the British Commonwealth, gather together every four years for a whole variety of different sports. Darryl's first assignment was weight-lifting. Unfortunately, a word-

A

for-word commentary would not capture the energy or the volume of his vocabulary, but he had you believing that what you were watching were the most outstanding feats that humanity had ever accomplished. I remember well, when one Australian of Bulgarian descent, had just won the gold medal, Darryl's voice could be heard reverberating across the room, 'They're going crazy here. Everyone's going crazy!' As the camera panned around the auditorium and the other competitors, it was very clear that no one was going crazy, except Darryl in the commentary box.

Later on in the week, they moved him to lawn bowls. This sport is not known as a ratings grabber. It is more often that not played by sports people who are reasonably conservative and consists of rolling a series of heavy balls very slowly along a long lawn to see who can get closest to the small white ball, or 'jack'. Yet, with Darryl commentating, this game took on epic proportions. Forget Ali and the 'Rumble in the Jungle,' move over Super Bowl, or the breaking of the world record in the 100 metre sprint; Lawn Bowls was here! So I sat glued to the

A

screen, and as I discovered afterwards, so did many of my friends, simply because of Darryl's enthusiasm. I too was jumping up and down when Sri Lanka defeated Barbados for one of the minor places. After all who couldn't be moved by such a sporting milestone!

Enthusiasm does that. It takes something that many of us would gloss over and injects it with new life. It has the ability to grip and to infect. Genuine enthusiasm can spread very quickly if hearts are open to its passion. Nothing is enthusiastic of itself, only people can be. Lawn bowls are not enthusiastic – Darryl is. As a result, those who are listening find their attitude changing, not from what they are seeing but from how they are seeing it.

ENTHUSIASM AND THE BIG PICTURE

Unfortunately we live in a world where this particular attitude is becoming endangered. People have begun to lose faith. They have stopped dreaming and believing and, like the fabled land in the <u>Never Ending Story</u>, are discovering the effervescence of life being eroded by the 'nothing'.

Our post-modern world, by and large, has decided that there is no such thing as truth, that absolutes need to be replaced by the quicksand of relativism. Therefore, concepts such as God, hope, meaning and self-worth have become just that . . . concepts. They are definitions of what we once believed and, as the madman declared in one of Dostoevsky's books, *'God is dead, and when He dies, we die.'* Now, I am not trying to get theological, but I must point out that this is one of the things that separates enthusiasm from mere hype. You see, enthusiasm is not simply generated by good things that happen, but rather by the realisation that we are involved in a good thing, called life, which has real meaning and real hope.

The word, enthusiasm, comes from the Greek, 'en theos', literally meaning, 'God within'. This is why Nihilism (the belief that there is nothing) inevitably leads to melancholy and despair. When God is not, then everything is meaningless. Or as Woody Allen put it:

A

'More than any time in history mankind faces a crossroads. One path leads to despair and utter hopelessness, the other to total destruction. Let us pray that we have the wisdom to choose correctly.'

This is one of the reasons why the individual who becomes convinced regarding the reality of the spiritual dimension, discovers in many cases an inner explosion of joy and enthusiasm. They are the logical conclusion to such a belief in the same way as foreboding and meaninglessness are those of its opposite.

ENTHUSIASM MAKES THE DIFFERENCE

In studying the life of Amazing Achievers, it is clear that it is enthusiasm that gives them the energy to push through to their dreams and see their objectives reached. Whether we are talking about Gandhi or Churchill, Florence Nightingale or Einstein, they all sensed there was meaning in what they were doing. They

A

were walking a road of destiny and the enthusiasm that such beliefs produce enabled them to finish the course. Regardless of what one does, it will be done better with enthusiasm. What causes people to succeed in life, receive promotions or discover opportunities, is not mere competence. The competent pass their exams and do what is required. The competent, who are enthusiastic as well, discover so much more.

If you are going to wash the dishes, 'whistle while you work'. If you are applying for a job, do it with a broad smile. If you are preaching a sermon, impart energy. If you are tucking your children into bed, make them feel that they are the most treasured children on the planet. If Helen Keller can talk about the beauty and joy of life, if a man who is paralysed can speak of life being a banquet, it poses the question as to why so many of the able-bodied and able-minded are emotionally and spiritually starving to death. The problem is not in surroundings, in jobs, marriages, or bank balances. The problem, and therefore the answer, lies within. Let us allow enthusiasm to change our worlds. Let us

A

live life with a sparkle in the eye and a skip in the step. After all, if we are on this road, we might as well take in the view and enjoy it rather than hurrying morbidly to our destination grumbling and complaining as we go.

A

CHAPTER 8

RED CARS TRAVEL TOGETHER

'THE ATTITUDE OF VISION'

The relationship between vision and attitude is both complex and co-dependent. Vision is all about how we see things, and how we see things, whether we like it or not, flows to us through the prism of our own perspective. Blake's poem we referred to earlier makes the important distinction between seeing with or through the eye. We are so familiar with the experience and sensation of sight that we can easily forget that the pupil is merely the porthole and the optic nerve

A

the cable. Sight takes place in the brain and is therefore subjective as well as objective. Our brain's job is to interpret the information so that we can understand what we are viewing.

I once saw a television interview with a lady who had been born blind. Due to advancing technology and the nature of her blindness she was able to regain full sight through a simple operation. Her story was fascinating. We can only wonder what it would be like to live for thirty years in a noise-filled world of darkness and then one day to suddenly discover the visual beauty of our surroundings.

Her guide dog took several weeks to work out what had happened to his mistress. She related the story of how one day, as he was eating his meal he began to eat the cat's food as well. She, on the far side of the room, shouted at him; the dog looked up amazed at this interruption in what must have been a decade-long habit. (No wonder that cat was so skinny!) The revelation of what this meant suddenly dawned on the labrador and he bounded over, jumped up on her chair and began to lick her face with delight.

A

What I found fascinating about the interview was her explanation of what it was like to have no visual information prior to full sight. She told how she was looking at a mug on the kitchen table, unable to work out what it was. Only when she reached out and touched it was she able to give the incoming pictures their right interpretation. She had the tactile information of what a mug is, but not the visual information.

Although most of us are not physically blind, we can be blind to opportunities, to potential and to reality, blinded by prejudice, resentment, previous experiences or lack of knowledge. Indeed, vision is the ability to see beyond the obvious, to see what others don't. As Kennedy pointed out, *'Eyes that look are common, eyes that see are rare.'*

I am firmly convinced that all of us can cultivate this attitude of vision, and as a result see life as it really is . . . intriguing and full of opportunity

A

YOUR EYES CAN LIE

One of our biggest stumbling blocks is that we have been taught to believe what we see. We think we see what actually is, and yet for a whole host of reasons this is not the case. Our brains are telling us what we see. In fact, what we see has as much to do with us as it does with the external world.

There are countless observations of this phenomenon, both from the world of experience and also psychology. G K Adams in M D Vernon's book, <u>Visual Perception</u>, cites such an example:

> *'I was looking out of the window, watching for the street car, and I saw through the shrubs by the fence the brilliant red slats of the familiar truck; just patches of red, brilliant scarlet. As I looked, it occurred to me that what I was really seeing were dead leaves on a tree; instantly the scarlet changed to a dull chocolate brown. I could actually "see" the change, as one sees changes in a theatre with a shift of lighting. The*

A

*scarlet seemed positively to fall
off the leaves, and to leave behind
it the dead brown. I tried to
recover the red by imagining the
truck, and found that I could
brown them somewhat; but I could
not get either the original scarlet
or the later dead chocolate. I went
out to see what the colour
"really" was, and found it to be a
distinctly reddish brown . . .'* [11]

The Rorschach Test is a good example of
this as well. Ink blots are put in front of
patients and they are asked to describe
what they see. What they see is not so
much a statement about the ink but a
statement about their own psyche;
something of who they are is projected
onto the scene which is then interpreted
and categorised. In short, we cannot fail
to mix ourselves into the picture. Like
jumping into the chalk drawings in Mary
Poppins, all of us become part of the
scenery. Life is not like visiting the
cinema, we are very much part of the
action.

I well remember, as a young child, going
to bed after an episode of <u>Dr Who</u> only

A

to see a monster on the back of my door. Yet, when the light went on the monster transmogrified into a dressing gown hanging on a hook. This monster, like beauty, was in the eye of the beholder. The important point to note here is that it is impossible for it to be otherwise. What this means, of course, is that as we change, what we see changes. As we grow, so does the expanse of our vision.

The pedantic fault-finders see the flaws because they are the only things that are in focus. You will bring them no satisfaction by fixing their small problems for they will continue to see only what is wrong. Nothing less than a change of heart will change their outlook. When I realised this, I stopped getting too upset over those who would continually criticise. The world has always had its Pharisees and their quibbling and negativity are merely a reflection of their dark and crippled souls. Jesus made this point well as he spoke about the fault-finders, who delight in pointing out the specks of dust in people's eyes while they have telegraph poles coming out of their own.

A

FIVE KEYS TO DEVELOPING VISION

NUMBER 1
PERSPECTIVE

There are many different ways I try to prove my masculinity. I like to arm wrestle 15-year-olds. I enjoy swimming in shark infested waters. (Just a Couple of Tips: If you are ever in a situation where there may be sharks in your vicinity . . . firstly, always swim with a friend and secondly, always carry a small knife. If a shark appears, pull out the knife, stab your friend and swim away!) I try to watch <u>Home Improvement</u> and mimic the guttural noises that Tim Allen makes; and lastly, I enjoy racing in Formula 1 cars in video game arcades. I especially enjoy the cars that are linked together, so you can race and triumph over your friend, your spouse or your six-year-old daughter!

I have noticed many of these car-racing video games have a variety of camera angles accessed by four buttons on the

A

left-hand side of the dash which allow you to change perspective:

- Camera 1 is a view that all of us have when driving a real car.

- Camera 2 is a camera mounted slightly further back in the vehicle giving a wider range of the road.

- Camera 3 is mounted on the back of the car, enabling you to see the cars beside you and almost your own entire vehicle.

- Camera 4 is a helicopter view above your car, enabling you to see not only the road ahead but what is around the bend as well.

I wish, in life, we all came complete with four camera angles and could, with the ease of pushing a button, get a different perspective. I wish, when I was having an argument with my wife, that she was able to hit Camera 4, zoom out and see that I was right! We do, of course, have the ability to change perspective but it takes training; it takes vision.

A

I was watching the news the other day and the reporter was speaking to people who had just lost their home and contents in a major bush fire. One lady, when asked how she felt, responded with a wry smile, 'Well, it could have been worse. We are alive and we were able to save the photographs. We can rebuild. Everything's going to be fine.' She had marvellously discovered the ability to go to Camera 4 and see things from a different angle.

This is unlike one man I heard about recently who was driving his new BMW along a coast road. He swerved to miss a truck and as a result rolled the vehicle several times. During one of the flips he was flung out of the window, just before the car fell 100ft to the rocks below and burst into flames. He stood shaking on the top of the cliff, and rather than being grateful that his life had been spared, he simply stood sobbing to himself, 'My new BMW, my new BMW!' The next car arrived and stopped quickly. The driver jumped out and ran up to the man and said, 'Sir, don't you realise you've lost your arm!' He had been so caught up with the loss of the car that he was unaware

A

that his right arm had been completely severed at the shoulder. He resembled the Black Knight in Monty Python's, <u>Holy Grail</u>. He then began to cry even louder, 'Oh no, my new Rolex!...' This is what I call losing perspective!

The concept of perspective is illuminating. It suggests that what we see is only partly right. If we could see it at a different distance, or from a different angle, or in a different way, we would have a more complete understanding of reality.

The park outside my window looks flat. From my perspective the world is flat. Yet we all know that if we were to ascend 100 miles, the curvature of the earth would reveal we were riding on a ball. Yet, for hundreds of years people believed the world was flat because they believed what they saw. They lacked the understanding that changed perspective gives. In fact, they were so convinced by what they saw that the plain evidence available to them was disregarded. The fact of the ship slowly disappearing over the horizon, or that the moon and other planets were round, or even the ancient

A

writings of scholars who had discovered the truth, like Ptolemy, were not considered. From their view of reality, which they took as the only view of reality - they had the truth; therefore all evidences to the contrary were conveniently ignored.

Amazing Achievers continually develop this attitude of vision by changing their perspective. Looking at problems in new ways. Coming at it from different angles. I like how General Abrams saw things in the American Civil War; down to his last 1,000 men his scouts reporting that they were completely surrounded by the enemy, he announced to his soldiers that he had good news. The good news was that they were now in a position that they could attack the enemy in any direction! The story is told today because with that kind of attitude, they did attack and won their battle.

I recently watched a documentary on the Harrier Jump Jet, the vertical takeoff plane that is used in many of the airforces around the world. The design is of British origin and the documentary was explaining how the Falklands War was

A

the jets' first real trial in battle conditions. Twenty Harriers were up against an Argentinean airforce of 200 planes. One of the British pilots being interviewed was asked how he and the other pilots dealt with the fact that the odds were very much against them. The interviewer remarked, '10 to 1 against, is not very encouraging.' The pilot merely smiled and said, 'We weren't bothered. We simply saw it as a "target rich" environment!' It was with that kind of attitude the fliers launched their sorties, and as a result the British air force did not lose a single Harrier in combat and yet inflicted major casualties on the enemy.

When the going gets tough, when the situation looks bleak, we must be able to train ourselves to reassess how we are viewing things. As we do, we will see new opportunities discover creative ways of solving problems and increasingly realise that how things first appear is rarely how they actually are.

A

NUMBER 2
KNOWLEDGE

Since vision is a mixture of who we are and what we see, a merge of the objective and the subjective, it therefore follows that the more we learn, the more we understand, the more our vision will be enhanced.

This can be observed, for example, in the study of art. A simple oil painting when merely glanced at yields little pleasure. Yet when one learns about the artist, the time in his life when the picture was painted, the things he was mulling over at the time, one begins to see the message of the work and to understand far more than the casual observer. Suddenly the picture tells a story and as a result becomes a better picture.

I had this experience when visiting a friend of mine in New Zealand. He had an early photograph of a man with sorrowful eyes and a black sooted face, looking down at the table at which he was seated. I asked him what the significance of this picture was. My friend began to explain that his grandparents had been

A

miners and that this was an early photograph of a common scene in many of the families at the time. The miner had just got back from his shift of twelve hours in the pits. The wife was probably about to serve the evening meal and normally, as the father returned from his shift, the sons would be leaving to take their turn underground. Life was simply a series of working, eating and sleeping, and the money earned just paid for the food and lodging. With this understanding, I could almost feel the melancholy and the despair that emanated from the man's eyes. What had been just an old photograph now carried a message. I saw it differently because I knew more.

> *'No one can understand the painted horse or bull unless he knows what such creatures are like.'*[12]

Meaningless scribble and strange shapes convey messages only to those who understand the language. A picture of a horse has no meaning if one has never seen a horse. There is nothing to identify it with. Hebrew is merely a mixture of shapes and dots until knowledge of the

A

Hebrew alphabet is gained. As we learn, so we see things differently. As we think about life, this attitude of vision is enhanced; focus comes and images that were on the periphery of our scope suddenly give input that we never picked up before.

Now, of course, this truth can be interfered with. It follows that faulty information will lead to faulty vision and upon this truth the world of propaganda has been built. Countries have gone to war with the backing of their population due to misinformation. The evil of racial prejudice was fueled for hundreds of years by faulty and agenda-filled theology. In other words, people didn't see those of different race as inferior to themselves by sight. It was that the brain, fed with knowledge that was erroneous, interpreted life in a way that made Apartheid a reasonable thing. Devious dogma can bend and warp the mind like a fair-ground mirror and, as a result, the distortion seen is mistaken for truth, and this 'truth' becomes the foundation for vitriol, meanness and even massacre. The clear-eyed, on the other hand, cannot see the

A

same image and as a result find such behaviour incomprehensible.

NUMBER 3
PERSISTENCE

Sometimes deeper vision is merely the result of continuing to steadfastly look. Rarely does the glance capture the detail. Many times it is only a fierce determination to continue to contemplate, that will finally yield the answer. Many of the world's great discoveries and scientific breakthroughs have taken place because of the considered. persistent stare. Newton declared he discovered gravity because he, *'thought about it all the time.'*

The Polish people have a saying, *'Sleep faster, we need the pillows.'* In other words, there are some things, like sleeping, that simply cannot be rushed. Sometimes continuing to look and patiently wait for revelation is a far surer path to answers than to allow the eyes to constantly dart back and forth frantically searching, yet continually missing.

A

When the 3-D Magic Eye illustrations first came out, it was not uncommon to see a whole crowd of people staring at a shop front window where one of these pictures was hanging. For many months, I thought the whole thing was a con. Obviously the pictures were simple patterns being marketed in a brilliant way. No matter how much I looked, I couldn't see what all the fuss was about. And what I couldn't see obviously couldn't be there.

One Christmas somebody gave me a whole book of these 3-D pictures. At this stage, I realised that my theory, that the whole thing was a sham, was probably not right, as there were an alarming number of people who claimed to have seen the light. Friends, relatives, people I trusted were all getting converted and so my frustration began to increase as my self-worth began to diminish. 'What is wrong with me? Why can't I see this?' So one day, with a steely look of determination, I grabbed the book, sat in my chair and resolved not to get out of it until I saw what all the fuss was about. It wasn't long, of course, until slowly but surely, floating triangles and dancing snakes began to appear before my very

A

eyes. Within a few minutes more I had turned into one of those obnoxious experts trying to convert the rest of my family into seeing what I had seen, and chiding them for their obvious ignorance and myopia.

Sometimes, the truth is only seen by the willingness to keep looking. Amazing Achievers, throughout history have had this doggedness about them. When others said it couldn't be done, or it wasn't there, they continued to look, scanning the horizon until their star appeared.

NUMBER 4
OPENNESS

We have already pointed out that reality may be different from our experience. How we see things today is partial. This is not only true in cosmic terms, in that *'we see through a glass darkly,'*[13] but also in the sense that sometimes, for whatever reason, we are unable to see what is plainly before our noses. I continually get frustrated when my wife points out where my car keys or glasses are, or discovers that lost sock in a drawer when, quite

A

clearly, when I had looked it just wasn't there.

The understanding, that what I see is not all there is to see, should encourage us to be more open minded. When we are convinced we know everything and then close our minds to every other permutation, light can no longer enter. It is the open mind that is able to gather information. Now, I am not saying here, what many who hold to the open-mind theory believe, that there is no truth and that all view points, all opinions are equally valid. I like what Chesterton said regarding the open mind, *'that it is like the open mouth and must be kept open until it finds something solid upon which to close.'* Openness is simply the awareness that no matter how clearly we see, we probably don't see at all. When new light comes it not only complements what we already know but it helps us get a broader picture and a more accurate understanding of that which lies before us.

On the other hand, it is true that life and circumstances can have radically different interpretations and sometimes we

A

experience a cerebral jolt when we cross over what is now referred to as a paradigm shift. This is where what we believed to be the case got turned on its head, and that which we observed was happening, and our subsequent interpretation of those observations, were flawed because our basic assumptions were wrong.

The best example I have heard of this is the story of a man, we'll call him Fred, waiting for a flight in a busy airport somewhere in the world. Fred decides to buy a bag of doughnuts while he is waiting for his boarding call. He purchases the doughnuts and goes to a table, places the bag of doughnuts on the table and then realises he would also like a cup of coffee. Fred returns to the counter, grabs a coffee, comes back to his table only to find another traveller sitting at the same table. The cafeteria was reasonably busy and so he thought nothing of it. He had a sip of coffee, reaches his hand into the bag of doughnuts and took one out. The man sitting the other side of the table looked up and smiled and then he too put his hand into the bag of doughnuts and took one out himself.

A

Fred could hardly believe his eyes. Here was a complete stranger helping himself, without even asking. Fred gave one of those withering looks and went back to reading the newspaper and sipping his coffee. After a while, Fred took another doughnut. This time, again, the other man reached in and took one as well. Fred bit his lip. He was about to say something but as he was composing himself an airport loud speaker announced a certain flight that was boarding, upon which the rude visitor at the table jumped up. He reached his hand one more time into the donut bag, took out the final doughnut, smiled at Fred, broke the doughnut in half, leaving Fred half and walked off. Fred was stunned. All he could do was sit there marvelling at the audacity of the man.

Soon it was time for Fred's plane to leave, he got up, picked up his coat and noticed that under his coat was a bag. He pulled it out. It was a bag of doughnuts. Suddenly in a flash he grasped that this was his bag of doughnuts! As the wheels slowly turned Fred realised that the man he had accused of eating his doughnuts,

A

was in fact, innocent. The reality was that Fred had been eating his!

NUMBER 5
DESIRE

The final factor in developing an attitude of vision has to do with what we wish. We see what we want to see. Bookshop hunters see bookshops wherever they go. Christians see evidences for God whilst atheists are continually turning up reasons that support their non-belief.

When I was in my late teens I lived in America for a year, after moving there from New Zealand. I was starved for news from my part of the world and was continually, both consciously and subconsciously, on the lookout for the words 'New Zealand'. One day, walking through a supermarket, my whole being was captured by a poster advertising New Zealand lamb. The words New Zealand had sprung out and hit me in the face. My American friends, who were with me at the time, didn't give the poster a second look.

A

We are all aware of this phenomenon. It's almost as if our brains go to work to point out that which we want to see. Look at the clouds and ask your children what animals they can observe and very quickly a series of camels, donkeys and of course, the mandatory sheep, will be quite obvious to everybody. If you were, however, to look at the same clouds, trying to see items of food for instance, arbitrary shapes would quickly be interpreted in different ways.

The brain is like a searchlight, continually on the alert for what we deem to be important information. It is constantly looking for what we want it to see. I never noticed the baby aisle in the supermarket until I had a baby. I was amazed at the amount of advertising for diapers and toddler toys. They had been there all the time. I just wasn't tuned into that frequency.

Children only see the funny pages in the morning paper. Teenage boys only pay attention to <u>Motoring for Sale</u> and the sports section. It's not that they see and choose not to read the rest, more often than not they simply don't see anything

A

else. As E H Gombrich put it, *'There is no such thing as the innocent eye, we are continually on the lookout, whether we realise it or not for what we want to see.'* Therefore, to change what we see we must grow in what we want to see.

We can look for problems or solutions, for reasons why we can't do something, or reasons why we can. Those that succeed in life tend to see life differently because they are looking for different things. Those that think money is evil will never see the possibilities of wealth that surround them. Those that see themselves as non-achievers will never see the opportunities that lie under their own feet.

Whether we win or lose, succeed or fail, has more to do with vision than it does with action. For action is merely the child of our vision. Amazing Achievers have spent the time and effort to develop this attitude of vision. They are like the prophets of old, the 'seers'. Their ability is not based upon some supernatural gift but upon the willingness to remove the internal blinkers, and to look so that they may truly see.

A

CHAPTER 9

LOSING MONEY IN MANHATTAN

'THE ATTITUDE OF HUMILITY'

There is nothing like a bit of humiliation to blow away bravado. We don't think of ourselves as proud but let us just suffer one embarrassing situation, and the truth is out. We are worried about looking good, having it all together, and being in control. We want to be well thought of, mentioned in knowledgeable conversation, welcomed when we enter the room, and glanced at admiringly by throngs of discerning teenagers. (Not that there is anything wrong with that I can hear Jerry

A

Seinfeld saying.) Self-effacement is not natural. Humility takes work. Pride, ego and self-assertiveness, on the other hand, flush themselves into our life at the touch of a button.

Pride causes me to blend when I am away from home. Tourists by perception are simple folk, bussed to and fro like ignorant swine, easy prey for rip-off merchants; they click their cameras furiously in the two minutes allotted before pouring into the sleazy, expensive, $100 under the counter to the driver, café. They are a happy flustered lot, drinking instant coffee and feasting on hamburger and fries. 'It's just like home,' is the highest recommendation that can be given, and then they are on their way again, leaving the locals looking on with nods of patronising bemusement.

Not me, however. No, in Paris, I will stand at the counter wearing my beret drinking a glass of Brouilly . . . in Venice avoid the Gondolas . . . in London the top level of double-deckers . . . cowboy boots for Texas . . . suit and tie for Rome . . . T-shirt for Brisbane - speak the language, catch the attitude, drink at the local.

A

Whether this philosophy works or not is another question, but I feel sort of smug as I travel . . . an undetected stranger in their midst . . . a citizen of the world . . . a cultural chameleon.

My motivation is two-fold. Firstly, to experience other countries one must put yourself in their shoes. No point eating at McDonalds when visiting Shanghai, instead find yourself one of those sheep-bladder restaurants and blend in. But I also find a lower darker motive . . . I want to be accepted, to be thought of as sophisticated, urbane, aware, and intuitive about my context. So I hide the guide book under my coat and refuse to ask for directions. In other words, what total strangers think of me is somehow important to my psyche. Pride governs my actions, often illogically so. For the most part, I am able to keep this awareness, that of my pride, out of sight and out of mind. Only when I get lost, commit a faux pas or am conned does my strong sense of humiliation throw a spotlight on this vice.

I remember many years ago, coming undone in Manhattan. I was enjoying

A

shouting at taxi drivers and snarling at foreigners who were face upward and continually bumping into me. In my wanderings, which were pretty extensive as this was my first visit, I became engrossed in a gambling game being played on the sidewalk. After watching for a few minutes, I worked it out and knew that here was my opportunity to make some money out of a few unsuspecting fellow New Yorkers. Within two minutes I had lost $200. I shrank physically and metaphorically down the alley and into the next block. I had been conned . . . me. What a fool, what an idiot . . . what a tourist! My devastation had more to do with lost confidence than it did money. My pride had set me up and the pain of the fall was protracted.

Such a small thing, yet pride has the potential to trip us up over the large things as well. Marriages, careers, companies and governments might well have been saved if the grace and power of humility were profiled a little more.

The word 'humility' to the contemporary ear seems quaint and archaic especially when it is mentioned alongside such buzz

A

words as self-esteem, confidence and enthusiasm. Probably more so today than at any other time in human history we are in the grip of what George Eliot called, *'unreflecting egoism'*. Pulitzer Prize Winner, Robert Coles, in his collection of essays, <u>The Minds Fate</u>, defines Eliot's term as, *'a driven kind of self-centredness that dominates a person's mental life.'*[14]

Indeed pride; like greed, has lost its stigma. Self-absorption is considered healthy, self-sacrifice, dysfunctional. This message is continually preached not only by our media but also by much of pop-psychology. Book titles like, <u>I'm Okay You're Okay</u> or <u>Look Out for Number One, Power, Pride, Possessions</u> have led the charge into narcissism. Narcissus, the young man from Greek mythology fell in love with his face as reflected in the lake. We would do well if we too 'watched ourselves', not in the sense of unfettered self-love but as a precaution against it. The truth is, of course, an attitude of humility, of service, or esteeming others more highly, leads to far greater fulfilment and achievement than an attitude of self-sufficiency ever could. Although this book may be, to the casual observer,

A

grouped within the genre of the frothy, banal and self-preoccupied that litter our best-selling lists, I trust that on closer inspection its message is more profound, more controversial, more countercultural.

There is nothing wrong with success, but success should impact beyond the life. It should make its mark on the marriage, the family, the country and the world. When we become our own end, we discover that the meaning of our story is absolutely pointless. As one wit observed, *'The person who is wrapped up in themselves, makes a very small package.'* The quality and attitude of humility are essential ingredients if we desire the ripple of our lives to extend outwards.

The task of maintaining humility is one that must be adhered to constantly. For the arch rival of this particular attitude is continually at the door, and when we begin to settle back and congratulate ourselves then pride begins to ooze its way in.

A

THE DANGER OF PRIDE

Since ancient times pride has been considered one of the deadly sins. Although it may lack the dark excitement of lust or greed, it is, nonetheless, the front runner in bringing misery into the human world. There are many reasons this is so. Here are just a few:

NUMBER 1
PRIDE PREVENTS GROWTH

When the head start swelling the mind stops growing. If I already think I know it, then my willingness to learn quickly disintegrates. It has correctly been pointed out that when we consider ourselves experts, we stop gaining expertise.

The nature of knowledge itself should make this point obvious. As the circle of information grows so also does the boundary of ignorance. Yet the reason the proud do not see this reality is that they are looking backward to what they have learned rather than forward to what is still unknown. The attitude is wrong because the perspective is wrong. And the

A

perspective is wrong because something has gone awry on the inside.

The humble are unafraid to keep learning for their hearts are sound. Apparent ignorance does not scare them because they realise they are far more than the sum of their knowledge. The attitude of pride, therefore, is a red light flashing. It underlies deeper problems.

NUMBER 2
PRIDE POISONS RELATIONSHIPS

Preoccupation with self by necessity implies less preoccupation with others. The greater my pride the harder it will be to build significant relationships. Marriage, for example, is all about giving of oneself to one's partner. The attitude of, 'what can I get out of this relationship?' fails to realise the spiritual law of giving and receiving, sowing and reaping. When I put others first I begin to discover myself. Yet when I focus on me alone, I lose more and more of who I actually am.

A

This explains why the givers in life have happiness and friends, whereas the takers usually have to spend the bulk of their income on trying to escape both their melancholy and loneliness.

NUMBER 3
PRIDE PRODUCES STRESS

Many times pride manifests itself by its 'need to be accepted and admired' by everyone else, and as a result spends a lot of its time worrying about how it looks, and what other people's impressions of it are. Most of worry evaporates when we learn how to forget ourselves. When one thinks about this it seems self-evident and so we imagine that the allure of this vice is easily combated. Just realise that pride is self-defeating and decide to work against its insistence. Yet it is here we discover another truth. The attitudes that will do us the most damage cannot be defeated by reason alone; they have hooked into our emotional world and to release ourselves from their grasp requires more than just a mental decision. We will need the help of friends beside and God above,

A

and we will also need to put our whole heart and soul into it. Then and only then can we begin to make progress.

NUMBER 4
PRIDE CREATES OPPOSITION

One of the reasons pride comes before a fall, is that the boasting swankering, self-promoter quickly fosters a secret desire in all those within earshot to see this moron eat his words. Watching the fall is fun and anything we can do to hasten its happening is encouraged.

On our High School bus we had a bully. His great delight was in terrorising us smaller kids and stealing any food that we might have. He was big and proud and not too smart. The wheels were turning, but the hamster was dead! So we hatched a plan, invested some of our hard-earned pocket money into the purchase of laxative chocolate which was then produced on the bus and consequently stolen and eaten. There was something wonderful about the success of our ploy.

A

The proud don't often realise that life works in this way. They create their own opposition, not realising that the misfortunes they suffer could have been avoided.

ON DEVELOPING HUMILITY

NUMBER 1
TAKE PERSONAL RESPONSIBILITY

The New Testament in several different places uses the phrase, *'humble yourselves'*.[15] The attitude of humility cannot be cultivated by merely changing the context of one's life. We may talk about humble circumstances but circumstances do not create humility. The inhabitants of shanty towns can be as proud as those in the palace. It has nothing to do with what you have but everything to do with what has you. Pride and humility are not the result of winning or losing, passing or failing. They are rather

A

the result of how we choose to interpret our life and its context.

NUMBER 2
EVALUATE YOUR STRENGTHS REALISTICALLY

There is a humorous anecdote told of a teenage boy speaking to his sister about how he is guilty of the sin of pride. His sister enquires as to how he has come to this conclusion. 'Well, every time I look in the mirror' he replies, 'I see my reflection and I think to myself, "What a hunk!".' To which his sister retorts, 'That's not vanity, that's ignorance.'

As in the story, other people help us view things more realistically. We all have gifts, talents and strengths, and humility does not ignore these, much less deny them. If you can sing well and say you can't then you are simply being untrue to yourself. The humble receive compliments with a simple thank you. They have realised that they may have strengths where others do not, but this in turn is balanced out by weaknesses in other fields of endeavour.

A

False humility, on the other hand, does no service to our world. It cowers from making a difference and what is worse does so under the guise of noble self-depreciation. Jesus spoke about not hiding your light. If we are meant to make this world a better place then it would be criminal to shrink from our potential. We have an obligation, I think, to be all we can be, to shine for all our worth. Not so that we are seen but that others might see more clearly.

One of my gifts is communication. I enjoy speaking to large crowds. The more the merrier and find I have the ability to communicate reasonably complex truths in a way that a majority of people understand. Yet, ask me to build a bookcase, thread a needle or change a tyre, and my steely confidence is quickly unraveled. I may be good at some things but I am absolutely terrible at others.

The best analogy of this necessary human interdependence is found in the New Testament. Community is described as being like a body. The body is made up of different parts, each has its function and yet all of them, individually, cannot

A

handle the task of living. Which limb is more important - the arm or the leg? If you had to lose one, which would you choose. I think most of us would prefer to keep them both intact! Different body parts resist comparison. They are different. Eyes can see, but ears can hear. We are not meant to choose between them but to celebrate the existence of both.

The corollary of this is, of course, that we also admit our weaknesses honestly. We understand that we can be both good and bad, heroes and villains, and that the crowd can either cheer or jeer.

I like what Winston Churchill once said when quizzed about his ability to maintain perspective and not let the events of his life and his amazing achievements go to his head. *'Well, I always remind myself,'* he said, *'when a large crowd turns up at any of my speeches that the crowd would be twice as large if I was to be hanged!'*

The humble understand this and therefore see themselves as part of a team. Happy to give and thrilled to receive.[16]

A

CHAPTER 10

LIFE IN A SIBERIAN PRISON

'THE ATTITUDE OF GRATITUDE'

There is nothing like sitting down to read a book and discovering in the process that you are being shaken to your core. Not many books have this ability but I experienced such a phenomenon recently. The book in question was Alexander Solzhenitsyn's, <u>A Day In the Life of Ivan Denisovich</u>.

The book follows a day in the life of a prisoner in one of the Russian gulags in Siberia. Within a few pages, partly due

A

to Solzhenitsyn's prose and partly due to the horror of the conditions being portrayed, one has a sense of the all-encompassing pain that such an existence entails; freezing conditions, hard labour, the fight for an extra crust of bread, the greyness of the Siberian landscape and the hopeless monotony. It saps one's energy and vigour just by reading about it.

It wasn't long into the book that I began to notice a distinct change in my attitude towards where I was and what I was doing. The cup of tea, which I had hardly given a second thought to, I now found myself deeply appreciating; the warmth of the air, my children playing in the pool, the smell of summer and our sense of freedom. There is nothing like the experience of learning of another's pain or misfortune to heighten one's own awareness of the many graces and gifts life presents to us all.

The final paragraph of the book caused this message to resound in my consciousness, even until now:

A

'Shukhov went to sleep fully content. He had many strokes of luck that day: they hadn't put him in the cells; they hadn't sent the team to the settlement; he'd pinched a bowl of Kasha at dinner; the team leader had fixed the rates well; he'd built a wall and had enjoyed doing it; he'd smuggled that bit of hacksaw-blade through; he'd earned something from Tsezar in the evening; he'd bought that tobacco; And he hadn't fallen ill. He'd got over it.

'A day without a dark cloud. Almost a happy day.

'There were three thousand, six hundred and sixty-three like that in his stretch. From the first clang of the rail to the last clang of the rail. The three extra days were for leap years.' [17]

Someone once said that the definition of a fortunate man is a man who thinks he is fortunate. Here, Ivan Denisovich has gratitude at the end of the day, while many

A

who are free and alive in Western society are depressed and embittered about the lives they lead. Yet they are alive, they are aware, and if they could just change their attitude, life would be wonderful.

Growing up in New Zealand, I attended Bream Bay College, situated in the farming town of Ruakaka in Northland. A small class, in a small school, in a small town. Yet three of my classmates died before they turned seventeen. One was driving on the Whangarei to Auckland road; coming down a thousand-foot hill, he decided to turn off the engine and coast to the bottom. As the first corner was reached, he realised the steering had locked when the ignition was off and consequently he plunged over the cliff in the darkness. Another was killed on a motorbike; another fell 150ft down a mountain . . . Yet I am alive, they are not.

This is the stuff upon which gratefulness is built.

Gratitude, like each one of the attitudes we are discussing, leads to other things. Some have even suggested that cultivating this particular attitude is the

A

most important, as it is the seedbed for all the others. Cicero is one such writer and, although we may not fully agree with his position, he bids us realise the importance of a thankful demeanour in life.

'For indeed, gentlemen, while I would fain have some tincture. (They don't use words like that any more!) Of all the virtues, there is no quality I would sooner have, and be thought to have, than gratitude. For gratitude . . . is even mother of all the rest. What is filial affection if not a benevolent gratitude to one's parents? What is patriotism, what is service to one's country in war and peace, if it is not a recollection of benefits received from that country?' [18]

THE CHILL OF DISCONTENT

'Striving to better, oft we mar what's well.' [19] *Shakespeare*

A

Without reminders of this sort, we can slowly begin to sink into an attitude of unreflective acceptance towards the wonders of life. The traffic is too noisy at night. The dishwasher has broken down. The dogs attacked the climbing rose or the flies are bad for this time of year. Such pettiness can quickly block our view. They are the fine print of life yet there is something about human nature that will turn such nuisances into headlines. It is only when we come face to face with real problems do we realise how we have been deceived.

This truth is evidenced by many who have faced the most difficult hardships throughout history and yet have exhibited this grace of gratefulness more than the rest. Again, this attitude is based upon the heart of the individual, not the problem they happen to be facing. There is simply too much to be thankful for to waste our time wallowing in self-pity. Gratefulness must be cultivated. We need to train ourselves to count our blessings. To be thankful for what is happening rather than dwelling on what is not.

A

A friend of mine who was a successful pastor used to sit on the stage during the first part of the service. As he would look out over the hundreds of people gathered, he would always notice who wasn't there and begin to wonder why that family or that person hadn't shown up on this particular day. By the time he was due to speak, he was completely depressed about the number of people who weren't there. One Sunday morning, as again he was noticing the latecomers and the absent, he sensed God speak to him, 'just be thankful that anybody turned up to listen to you at all!' In this case, he was overlooking the fact that some 700 people had turned up to be part of the service. That which we do not have speaks louder to us than the graces we enjoy. It is the absent crowd that heckles the most, while the joys of life that surround us speak softly and are easily ignored.

Amazing Achievers then, regardless of their circumstances, can always muster a smile. They may not be satisfied but they are content. They will always have more to do but inwardly they are at peace. They are called rather than driven. They want what they have and refuse to spend

A

their life in what K D Lang called, *'constant craving'*. They ensure that they live today rather than deciding to live at some unfixed point in the future; a time when they have the new car, the new job, the new pool or new marriage. Life must be lived in the moment in appreciating and being grateful for how things are right now.

A few months ago I was driving to an evening meeting when I passed by a small building belonging to the S.I.D.S. Foundation. S.I.D.S stands for 'Sudden Infant Death Syndrome'. What caught my eye was a family who were walking up the main stairs, the husband and wife holding hands followed by what was probably a five year old little girl clutching a teddy bear. I realised that the only reason they were entering the building was probably to attend the evening support group held for families who had lost a child.

My heart went out to them and my thoughts turned quickly to my own family of three wonderful girls. Three girls, I might hasten to add, whom on that particular day I had not exactly been

A

cherishing. They had annoyed me. The constant noise, infighting and general lack of speed to do what I asked them . . . yet suddenly all of this was forgotten. They were alive. They were wonderful. That night I went into their rooms and watched them as they were sleeping, quietly praying and asking God to forgive me for my attitude, softly giving thanks for the privileges and joys that He had so graciously sent my way.

A

A

CHAPTER 11

HAVE MY SEAT YOU MISERABLE #?*◎!

'THE ATTITUDE OF GENEROSITY'

'HE WHO TENDS THE FIG TREE
WILL EAT OF ITS FRUIT.'

PROVERBS 27:18

It would be foolish to think that the age of greed finished at the end of the 1980s with the Wall Street crash. The power of materialism continues to linger wherever there is a buck to be made or a fortune to be seized.

A

Yet, I am constantly encouraged by the new literature concerning financial management and investment philosophy that continues to grow year by year. There are, of course, always the superficial and vulgar offerings to the power of money. These can be camouflaged with Christian theology or pitched as the latest scientific breakthrough, <u>How You Too Can Make a Million Dollars Within a Year by Buying this Book</u>.

I say I have been encouraged because this has not been the tenor of many books that have been published recently. More and more commentators are beginning to point out the truth generations have understood, that not only does giving lead to getting, but there is no point getting unless you intend to give. Books as varied as Robert Kiyosaki's <u>Rich Dad Poor Dad</u>, Anthony Robbins' <u>Awaken the Giant Within</u>, or the more recent best seller, <u>The Millionaire Next Door</u> by Thomas Stanley and William Danko.

What all these books have in common, apart from a pragmatic view of financial management, is an emphasis on generosity. The importance of giving

A

away, not just money, but time, effort, energy and friendship as well. That life is about what we can give not what we can get. When it comes to generosity these authors are not just talking about giving in some kind of arbitrary way but in a planned percentage approach to giving. Tony Robbins puts it this way,

> *'Remember the power and value of tithing. I can tell you that my financial world began to turn around the day I gave a little more than $20 to someone, when I really didn't have the $20 to give . . . most people say I'll tithe when I have more money.*

> *'Which do you think would be more difficult to do, to give a dime out of a dollar or give $100,000 out of a million? The answer is obvious . . . I'm not suggesting that 10% is a figure that should be etched in stone but do make a commitment to take a portion of what you earn and give it in a way that gives you joy. The beauty of tithing is that by giving away a portion of what you earn you are*

teaching your brain that you have more than enough. You'll be beyond scarcity, and that belief system alone will change your life.'[20]

Christian churches have taught the principle of tithing for generations and it has proven to be so counter-cultural that commentators often bring its practice up as a reason to not only dissuade people from church attendance but from taking the very message of Christianity seriously at all. It has been true that various financial scandals in the church world have not helped, and yet the concept of tithing is solid and liberating. This is seen clearly when you compare it to the other messages that contemporary society is communicating.

Probably the main one that we all have to face is that which the banks and the retailers enthuse about daily. Namely, spend 110% of what you earn and borrow the extra using the wide selection of short-term credit options. This particular message has been plugged so much that it now seems reasonable. Compare this to the biblical guidelines to finance,

A

which is use 90% of what you earn to live. By doing this you have more than enough to give back into churches and other non-profit organisations that have the mandate to change society by working to change people from the inside out and to minister practically to the hurts of society.

When put in this light, the principles of giving seem, because they are, eminently reasonable.

Generosity does far more, however, than benefit society in this practical way. It actually releases finances to the generous person. Whether we call this sowing and reaping, giving and receiving or the law of attraction, there is something about this kind of attitude that enriches its owner in a wide variety of ways.

One does not give to get, yet giving begets getting. An attitude of generosity seems to trigger something. It is almost as if the world begins to work in your favour. An old English proverb puts it this way, *'The hand that gives, gathers.'* Notice we are not primarily talking here about the act of giving but the attitude. You don't have to be rich to be generous. To give a little

A

with joy amounts to far more than giving a lot grudgingly or with pious self-congratulation.

Now don't get me wrong; writing this stuff is easy. Doing it is another question. Probably the greatest pain in writing a book like this is the leverage it gives to my scruples. 'Go on, leave a larger tip. You wrote the chapter. Remember?'

The area I find the most difficult, however, is generosity in the 'inner plane, long flight, personal space department.' I fight for the aisle seat and then do deals with flight staff on keeping that middle seat free. The worst fate is to find myself, due to a computer glitch, nasty steward, or 'God's just trying to give me a miserable day,' . . . in the middle seat, with an overbearing salesman on one side and an overweight, under-showered individual on the other. At times like this my fight for space becomes desperate.

First remove all flight magazines from the sleeve in front of your seat and then put them surreptitiously in the sleeve in front of the salesman. (Wait until he has clambered over you and gone to the loo,

A

which knowing your luck will be every ten minutes.) This gives you an extra 0.8 mm of room!

Secondly, the arm rests. Keep your arms on both of them at all times. If you haven't noticed there are only four arm rests to go between six arms. So mentally block out that itching on your head and ignore that urge to blow your nose. Let it run down your face but whatever you do don't give territory to the enemy.

Thirdly, put the headphones on immediately. This sends the message I don't want to talk to you and I certainly don't want to listen to you. I would prefer to hear a documentary on moles or the latest collection of country music (is that an oxymoron?) through the powerful, crystal clear, non-Dolby ear plugs.

Now I am not always this bad . . . maybe I am. But slowly I am learning this truth of generosity. It is a little bit like the quote from the film, <u>What Dreams May Come</u>: *'Sometimes when you lose, you win.'*

Just the other day on a flight from Sydney to Perth, I had not only got myself the

A

desired aisle seat, but had (due to my Frequent Flyer status and sycophantic grovelling) been able to have the middle seat 'blocked off'. These two words are amongst the loveliest couplets that flight staff can utter. (Not of course, to be compared with the most wonderful words in the English language, 'upgrade' or 'first class' or 'the almost orgasmic combination of these two as in, 'would you mind if we upgraded you to first class?')

So here I was, the doors were closed, the plane was about to leave the gate when I heard one of those interfering, insensitive flight stewards saying, 'Here's a seat.' I looked up, realising that my coveted prize of a free middle seat was about to be ripped from my grasp, to see a giantess. I kid you not. She was the centre for the state basketball team and was being moved from her cramped back row to mine due to her six-foot nine frame. Well thank you very much! My dark mutterings were not heard by the flight attendant who was no doubt delighted with his 'good deed' for the day. My stingy attitude meant for the next five

A

hours I felt unfairly treated and refused to speak a word to the lady on principle.

The very next flight I was on, I found myself aisle seat, sitting next to a man who had been separated from his wife and baby who were sitting across the aisle from me also in a middle seat. What bad planning I thought when suddenly the still small voice of conscience began to suggest I give up my seat for hers. Cold sweat broke out on my brow as I contemplated the hideousness of this suggestion. Yet ten minutes later I found myself exchanging seats. I could hear the inner voices jeering, 'It's your own fault for writing books about this stuff.' Yet I must admit, that flight was great. The look of thanks from the young mother, the surprise and grudging admiration of the man now sitting next to me on the aisle (who had refused to give up his seat when asked when they first boarded) and the overwhelming sense of peace and pleasure.

Now although I am not on the lookout for middle seats and still enjoy a little bit of room, I learnt a valuable lesson that day. That the generous win and the stingy miss

A

out. My world grew larger even though my seat was more cramped.

This spirit of generosity, once released, will pervade our whole life. We move beyond simply giving what we have and begin to give of who we are. As a result, life becomes richer. Dickens story of Scrooge is one clear example of this but I will probably give the last word to Winston Churchill who said, *'We make a living by what we get but we make a life by what we give.'*

A

EPILOGUE

'OBJECTIVE LIFE
CIRCUMSTANCES HAVE A
NEGLIGIBLE ROLE TO PLAY IN
A THEORY OF HAPPINESS.'[21]

RICHARD KAMMANN

A

A

Tangibility is king when it comes to grabbing our attention. Good looks, money in the bank, political clout or popular appeal seem more real to us. They are obvious and tactile, easily measured and quickly seen. It is little wonder, therefore, that the intangible world of attitude is so often neglected. It finds itself in the blind spot of a contemporary society whose focus is on 'concrete reality'.

Yet, as we have discussed, the major component of success, happiness and zest for living comes from how we perceive our world and ourselves. This miracle of attitude, this key to life change will be lost to our consciousness if we do not keep its truth constantly before our eyes. Like adding fuel to the car, we all need regular and generous attitude top-ups. Not only what I do but how I do it, not only what I give but how I give it. Such maxims must become our mantra.

Knowledge and competence are all very well but leave them without the power of attitude and life loses its sparkle. The older I get the more I realise this truth. I, like anybody else, can still get a lousy attitude but I cannot claim ignorance as an excuse. I know that to allow my life to be dominated by the negative side of the attitude equation, is totally counter-productive. I will hurt those around me, my heart and mind will shrink and my dreams and destiny will be hindered.

So in the final analysis the wisest thing, as the prophet 'Nike' has declared, is do it with attitude.

ENDNOTES

1   BLAKE, WILLIAM, THE EVERLASTING GOSPEL,
    COMPLETE WRITING OF WILLIAM BLAKE , LINES
    103-106, EDITED GEOFFREY KEYNES, OXFORD
    UNIVERSITY PRESS, LONDON, 1966, PG. 753

2   PSYCHOLOGY TODAY, JUNE 1975 AS QUOTED BY
    DENISE WINN, THE MANIPULATED MIND,
    OCTAGON PRESS, LONDON 1983, PG. 110

3   THE BULLETIN MAGAZINE, AUSTRALIA,
    DECEMBER, 1998, PG. 20

4   ZIGLAR, ZIG, SEE YOU AT THE TOP, PELICAN
    PRESS

5   THE POETICAL WORKS OF WILLIAM BLAKE,
    LONDON, OXFORD UNIVERSITY, 1905, PGS. 286-95

6   SONG OF SOLOMON, CHAPTER 2, VERSE 15

7   JEREMIAH CHAPTER 12 VERSE 5

8   PROVERBS CHAPTER 4 VERSE 23

9   NUMBERS CHAPTER 13 VERSE 33

10 MONTY PYTHON, 'LIVE AT HOLLYWOOD BOWL'

11 AS QUOTED BY E H GOMBRICH, THE SENSE OF
    ORDER, PHAIDON PRESS, OXFORD, 1979, PG. 189

12 PHILOSTRATUS, LIFE OF APOLLONIUS OF TYANA,
    BOOK II, CHAPTER 22 AS QUOTED BY E H
    GOMBRICH, ART AND ILLUSION, PHAIDON PRESS,
    OXFORD, 1982, PG. 155

13 1 CORINTHIANS CHAPTER 13 VERSE 12

14 ROBERT COLES, THE MINDS FATE, LITTLE BROWN
    & COMPANY, BOSTON, 1995, PG. 87

15 1 PETER CHAPTER 5 VERSE 7

16 I AM INDEBTED TO JACK HAYNES, LEADER OF A
    CHURCH IN PENRITH, NEW SOUTH WALES,
    AUSTRALIA, FOR A MESSAGE HE PREACHED ON
    'HUMILITY', FROM WHICH I GLEANED SOME OF THE
    SUBHEADINGS I HAVE USED IN THIS CHAPTER.

17   SOLZHENITSYN, ALEXANDER, ONE DAY IN THE
     LIFE OF IVAN DENISOVICH, PENGUIN BOOKS,
     1963, PG. 142

18   PRO CNAEO PLANCIO, CHAPTER 33, SECTION 80,
     THE LOEB CLASSICAL LIBRARY, THE SPEECHES OF
     CICERO , WILLIAM HEINEMANN, LONDON, 1955,
     PG. 513

19   SHAKESPEARE, WILLIAM, KING LEAR, SCENE 1,
     ACT 4, LINE 347

20   ROBBINS, ANTHONY, AWAKEN THE GIANT WITHIN,
     SIMON AND SCHUSTER, NEW YORK, 1992, PG. 469

21   MEYERS, DAVID, THE PURSUIT OF HAPPINESS,
     COLLINS PUBLISHERS, LONDON, 1993, PG. 47

A

ABOUT THE AUTHOR

Phil Baker is one of Australia's leading speakers, who has the ability to combine solid content with a practical, humorous and dynamic delivery.

He is also the author of several other books, including:

- The Best Seller - Secrets of Super Achievers

- Wisdom – The Forgotten Factor of Success

Having been born in England, raised in new Zealand, he now resides in Perth, Western Australia where he pastors a contemporary church, Riverview Church, Burswood, which attracts over 2000 people every Sunday.

Phil is married to Heather and they have three girls, Jazmin, Temily and Isabel.

A

NOTES

NOTES

NOTES

NOTES

NOTES

NOTES

NOTES

NOTES

NOTES

NOTES